CONNECTICUT

Quaint, Historic Barns and Farms of the Nutmeg State

Christina E. Cole

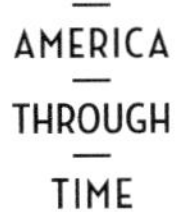

AMERICA
THROUGH
TIME

America Through Time®
www.through-time.com

First published 2025

ISBN 978-1-62545-157-6

Typeset in 9pt on 13pt Gotham
Printed and bound in England

Foreword

When I travel across Connecticut, my attention is sometimes diverted to the number of stone walls dotting the perimeters of roads and highways. They are some of the last remains of a bygone time when farms covered most of the land.

By the mid-1800s, many Connecticut families depended on farming for their livelihoods. Today, Connecticut has over 5,000 farms. The commodities they produce include fruit, vegetables, dairy, and fish, along with seasonal agritourism ranging from pick-your-own to pumpkins and Christmas trees. In recent years, the number of breweries and wineries cropping up has enriched the Connecticut landscape.

You don't have to travel far to find evidence of the state's agricultural history. Regarding barns, Connecticut serves as a delightful palette to the eager observer. Many of these places are set in beautiful landscapes worthy of picture-perfect moments. From barns and silos to hillsides and pastures, these surroundings set a backdrop for the imagination to wander to any time in history.

Christina's photography does just that—each frame captures the essence of a moment in time to be defined by the viewer. One example is her view of West Rock, which mimics the famous 1849 Frederic Edwin Church painting—though over a century and a half later, her depiction makes it seem as though time stood still.

Christina is a natural explorer. Her boundless bravery follows the road less traveled, revealing "weird, wild, and wonderful" treasures—from a far-off shed to a forgotten outhouse. The images she captures there take us to places we might never find on our own, and her curiosity plays an integral part in the treasures she uncovers.

I am always awestruck by the lighting in her photographs. Her use of natural light creates long shadows from light spilling through windows and doorways. Dramatic and defined clouds edge the skies in her landscapes—giving the sky as much prominence as the photograph's main subject. In some instances, a golden aura from the early morning or late afternoon sun is cast on her structures, creating a soft, warm glow. Without these ingredients, these renderings could be rather dull.

But dull and boring are words that should never be associated with Christina—or her work. She is enthralled by any adventure and finds beauty in even the oddest things. Her fascination with the find captivates her daily life. Whether unearthed by her hands or discovered through her lens and captured within a frame, this curiosity of exploration and characteristic of caring makes her the perfect witness to history.

Some might look at a barn and think of it as just a worn-out old building, but barns take us back to our agricultural roots. Sadly, many of these old rustic buildings are disappearing and, perhaps, much of the history that is held within. In this book, Christina's photographs help to preserve the history and traditions of these unique places and keep each building or structure as a historic fixture in a particular time and place in our lives.

Lori D. Golias

Lori D. Golias is an Emmy and Edward R. Murrow award-winning television photojournalist who has been covering Connecticut for over twenty-five years.

Contents

Acknowledgments

This book is dedicated to David Hamilton Graham from 12-10-1980 to 12-29-2023 AND 01-16-2024. My forever companion and love. This book and ten years of happiness, love, and adventures would not have been possible without him. I will grieve you until I follow you into the after.

Thank you to all the farm owners and people who let me invade their lives and squeeze their critters to get these stories and pictures.

A special thank you to my editors and publishers, who always took a chance on my wild ideas and gave me extra time when my life changed drastically in 2023. I did not think I would complete this book, and they gave me the time to persevere.

Thank you to all the true friends and family who were there for me during the most traumatic part of my life. Those who treated me as family and did not discard me with David's passing. This, and all its beauty, is for you.

And, of course, my daughter, Addison Lainey Guin, who mesmerizes me with her continuous achievements, creativity, and beauty. I love you.

Introduction

The book's original concept was to show how farms and their decorative structures had evolved from their essential purpose to sustainable modern ventures. The first year brought lush, abundant produce with several unique farm stands and thriving fields. It would be easy; I would revisit what I missed next season. Covid came into effect, and a saturated period thwarted farmers' best efforts. I pushed the book back for fall, then spring, and those too had problems: draught. Again, farming is falling behind, leaving barely anything for the consumer. Year three of trying to get the gist in pictures was countered by people losing their livelihood and no interest in strangers coming around during a pandemic. A hobby farm of Babydoll Southdown Sheep ghosted me. Per the Southington postman, the oldest barn in Connecticut has been under restoration construction for numerous years and will probably never be finished. Sustainability was becoming a daily part of our language; memes about millennial trust children raising salamanders and working 38.1279 hours while becoming millionaires have become permanent fodder. At inception, Connecticut's farm industry totaled 5,000 farms. The end of the project has only raised 521 more. Agriculture is a 4-billion-dollar industry in its small 5,018 miles, making up 22,000 of Connecticut's jobs. More and more people are seeing the importance of growing their food, primarily due to the rising cost of groceries and lack of fresh produce. Then tragedy struck, and I lost my best friend and significant other unexpectedly. It did not seem as important to release a book about vegetables and pretty structures. It has taken me four years to conclude this chapter, which I think he would have wanted me to, considering I dragged him along to all the locations when he could have been composing or playing music. Therefore, I dedicate this book to a wonderful, giving man who never said no, hoping that others find it as enchanting to read as we did discovering the places featured in it.

1

Halfinger Farms' Pick-Your-Own Dancing Daffodils

Local is Better; you leave with lifelong friends instead of just a business transaction.

Jenn Halfinger, part owner of Dancing Daffodils, will tell you that the Daffodil Farm is their joy! Who knew this yellow ambassador of spring could possess such goodness and power? No farms, no flowers. The farm has allowed Jenn to live with her family and, as she puts it, "Sometimes selfishly revel in happiness too with the guests." Dancing Daffodils and Halfinger Farms allowed her to be home when the bus rolled in and have the power of choice on when and how to work.

"Farmers are tough people. Need a good employee? Hire a farmer! "Jen says, "Sometimes I walk into the greenhouses and am still astounded by how beautiful they are." I, the author, would get 3 AM calls from Jenn to see the moonlight over the fields of daffodils and witness her daily splendor. Jenn often says she gets taken aback momentarily by the area's beauty before falling back into grower mode again and looking for issues. She thinks, "Where did twenty-nine years go? We were supposed to start down flapping, and then the daffodil farm happened. I also think that John, my husband, must be so proud of all he has accomplished without the layers of family support and a real budget! He is an example of a salt-of-the-earth tough guy! The real, true machismo!" They are both salt-of-the-earth and a massive part of what I miss about Connecticut and the area I lived in. The farm has a pick-your-own daffodil hotline for 'dil and weather updates at 860-345-4609 to verify the picking status.

Daffodils are from the genus Narcissus. Narcissus is the Latin name for daffodil. Narcissus is the birth flower for December, and my favorite bloom is precocious. That information is just in case someone wants to send a truckload to Maine. There are thirty-six species of the 'dil. The sure sign of spring, daffodils symbolize hope, rebirth with new beginnings, and good luck.

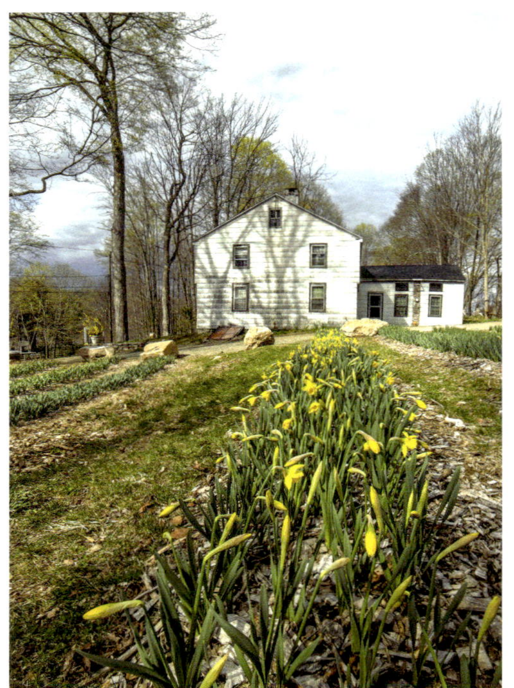

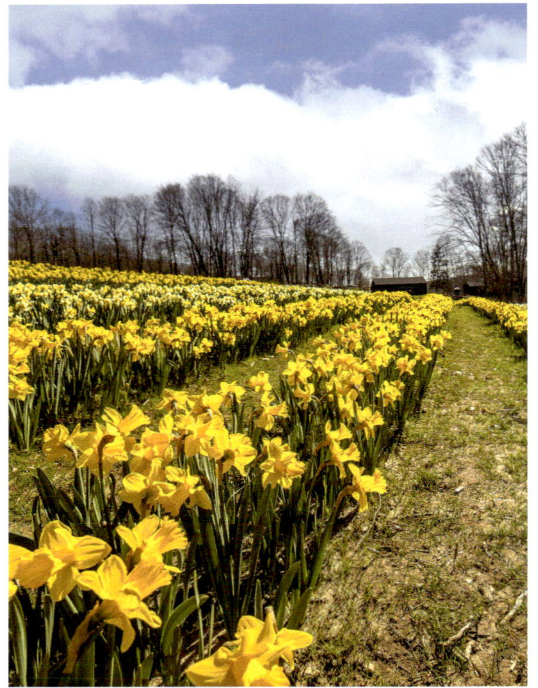

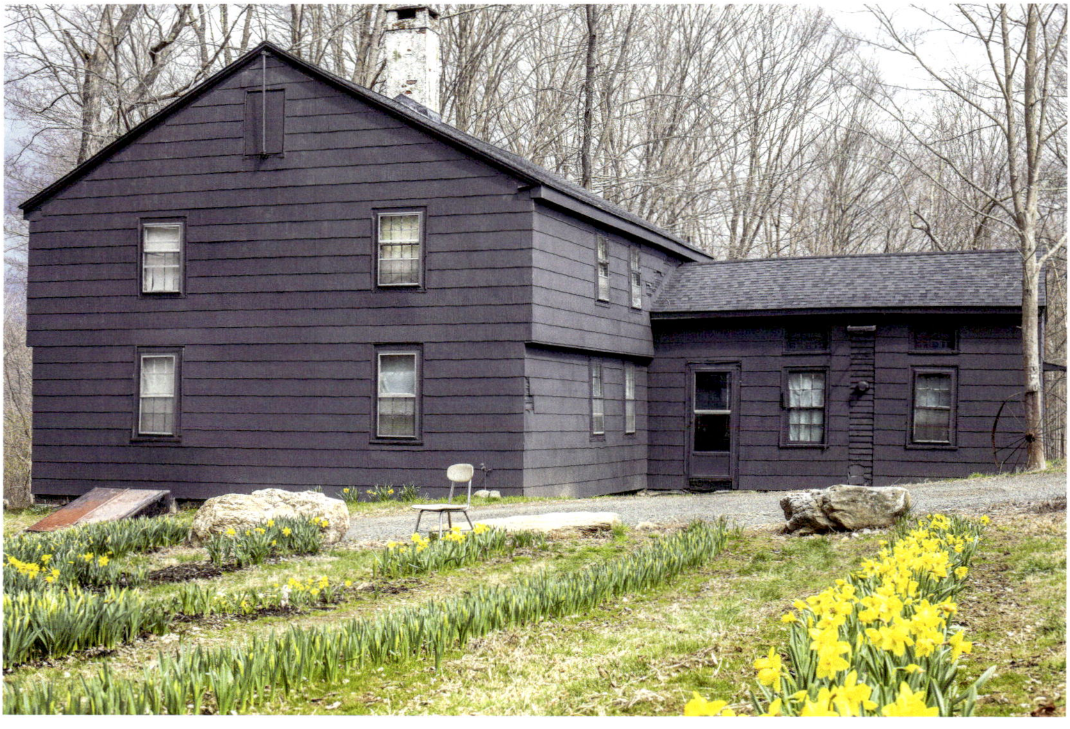

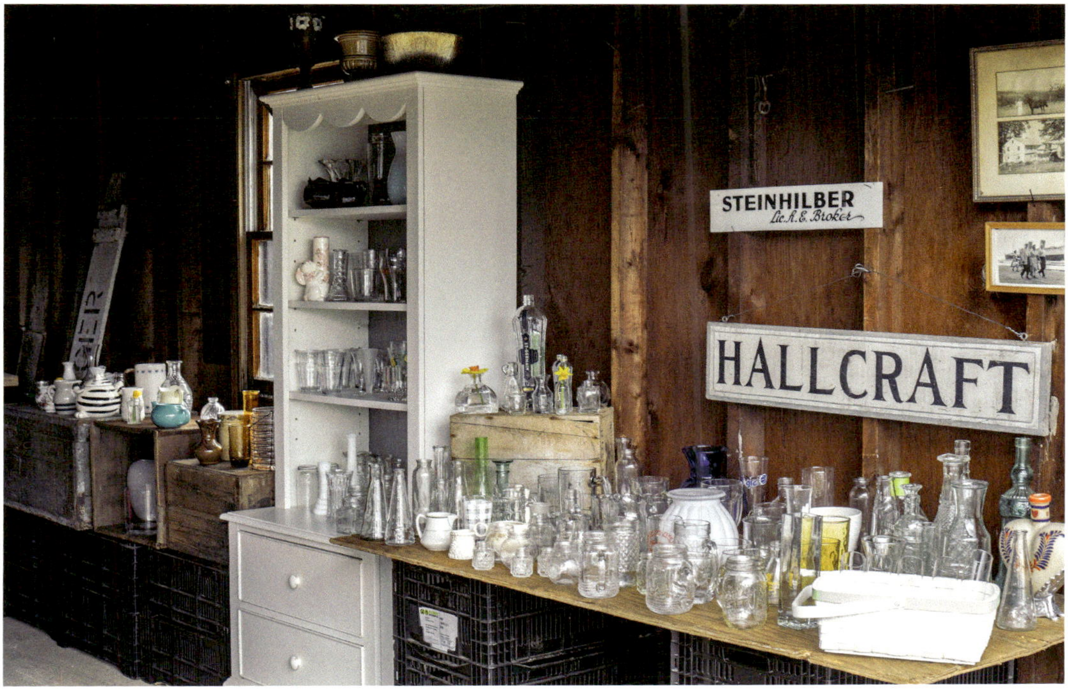

STEINHILBER
Lic. R. E. Broker
HALLCRAFT

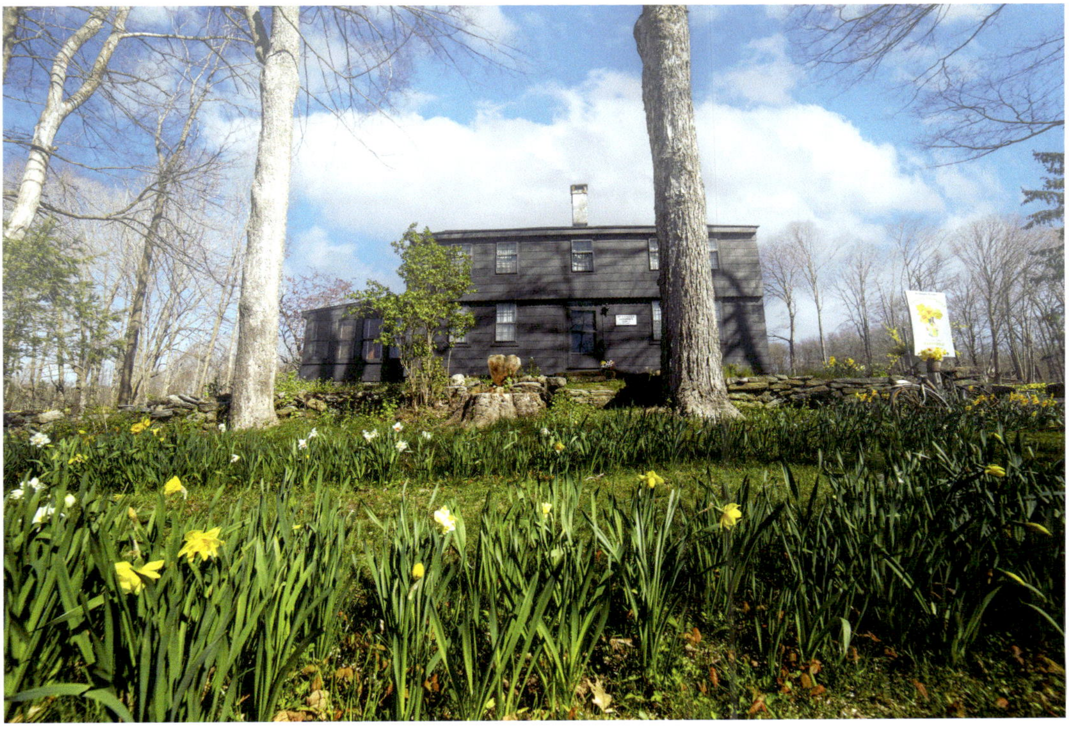

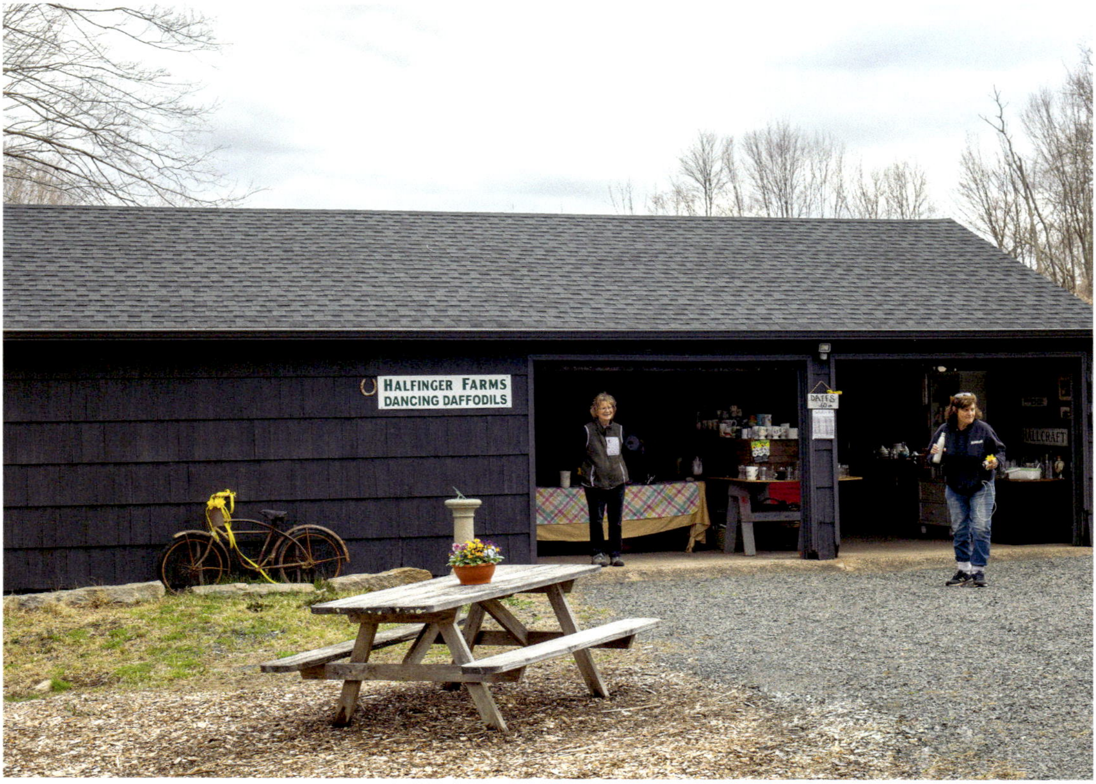

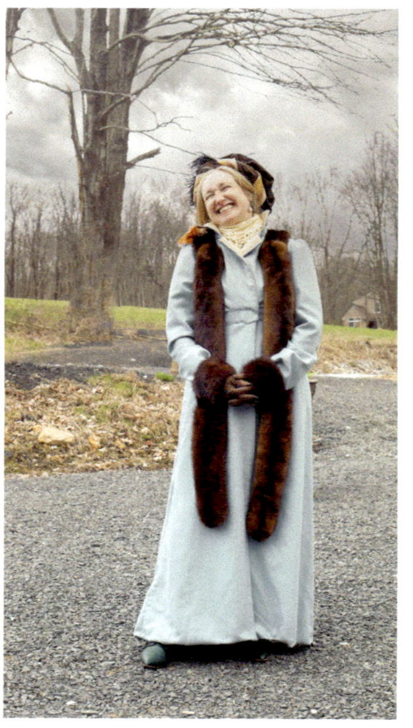

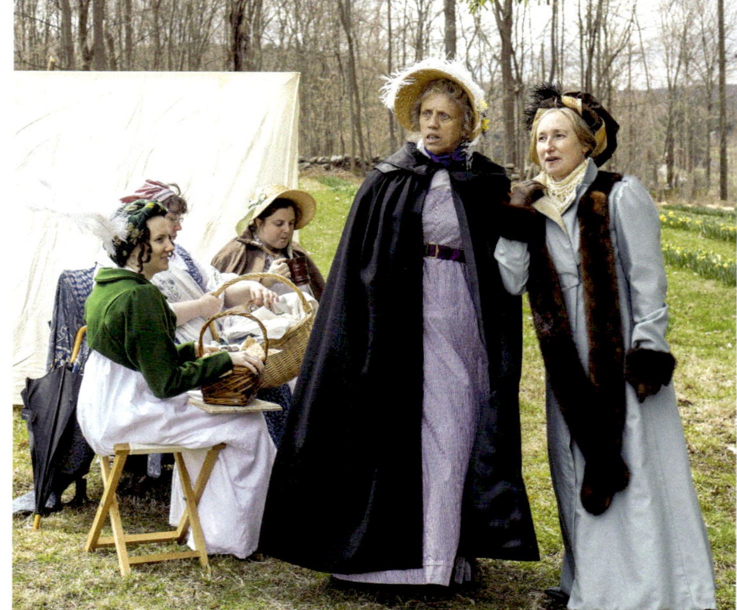

2
Wicked Tulip Farm, Preston

A million and a half tulips are planted with a tractor versus the 60,000 by hand, husband and wife team Keriann and Jeroen Koeman started with. The colder climate of Connecticut is reminiscent of Jeroen's Dutch roots in the Netherlands and makes for the perfect growing conditions for their dream of owning a tulip flower farm.

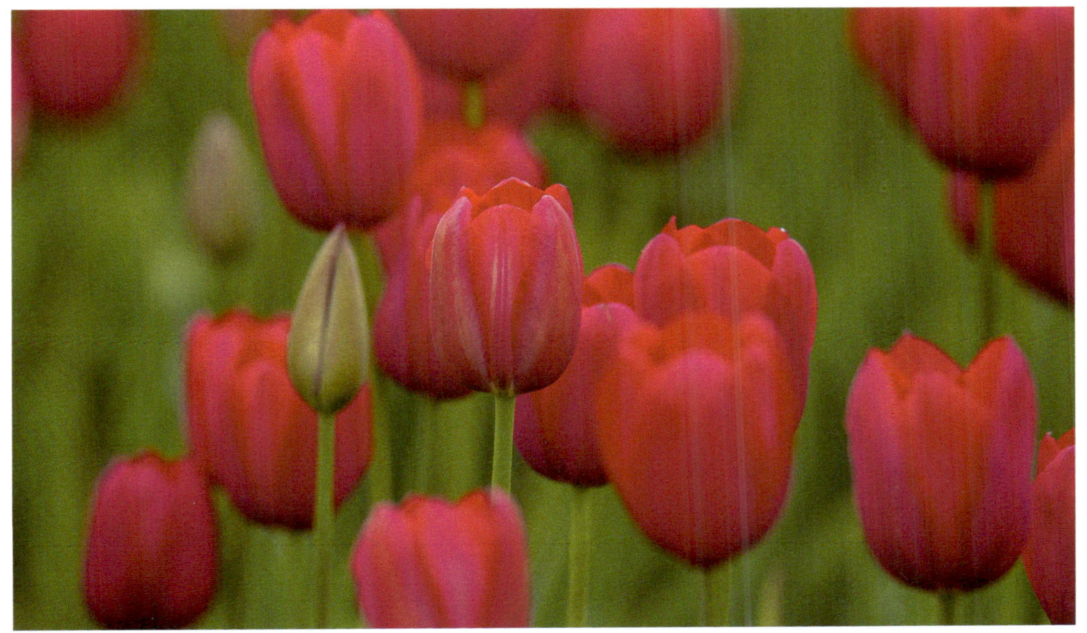

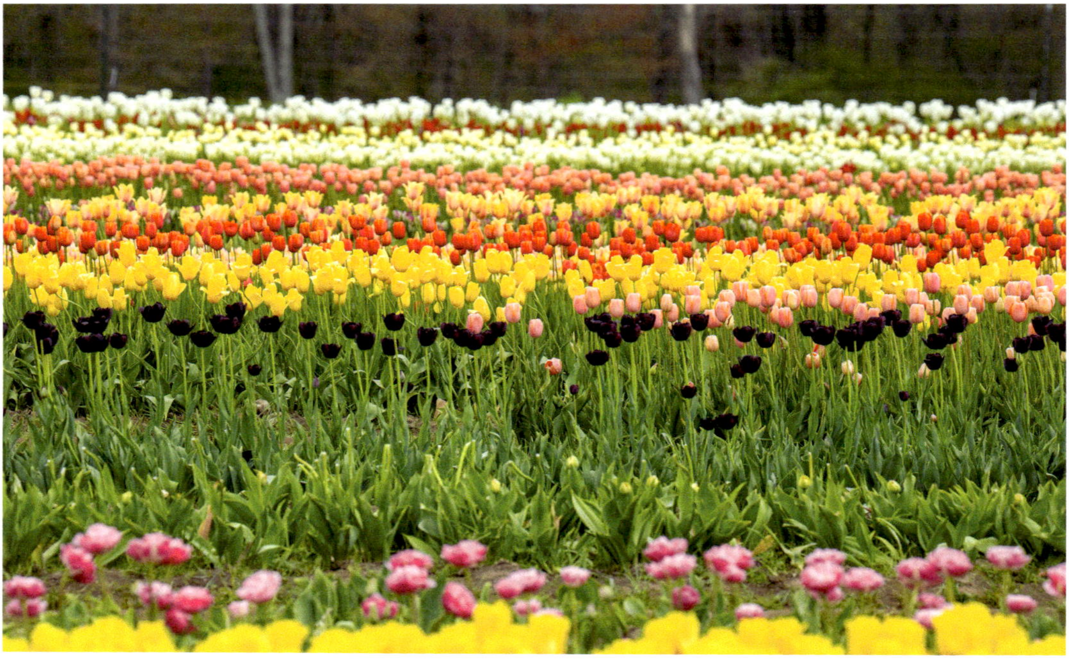

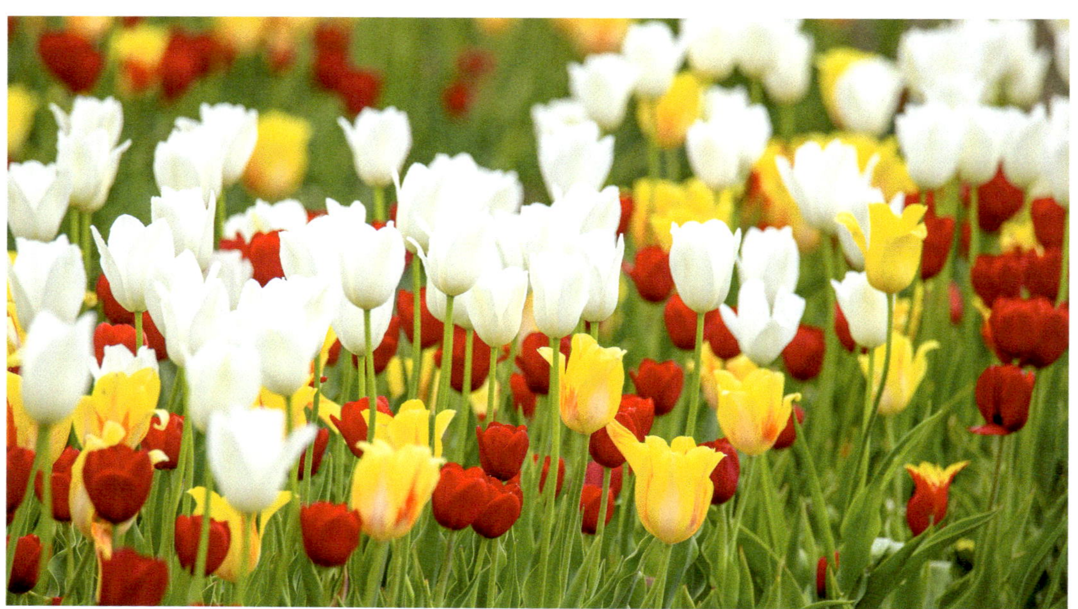

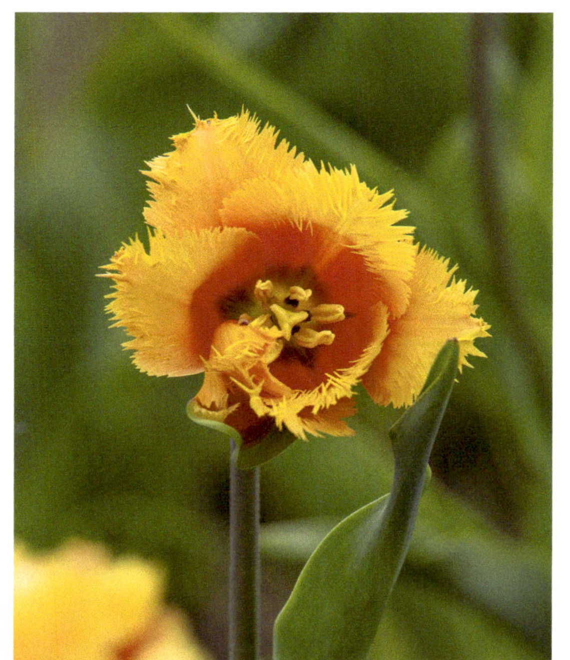

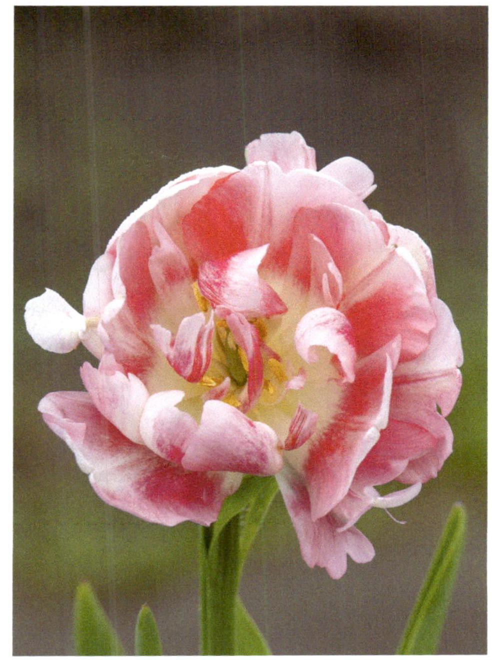

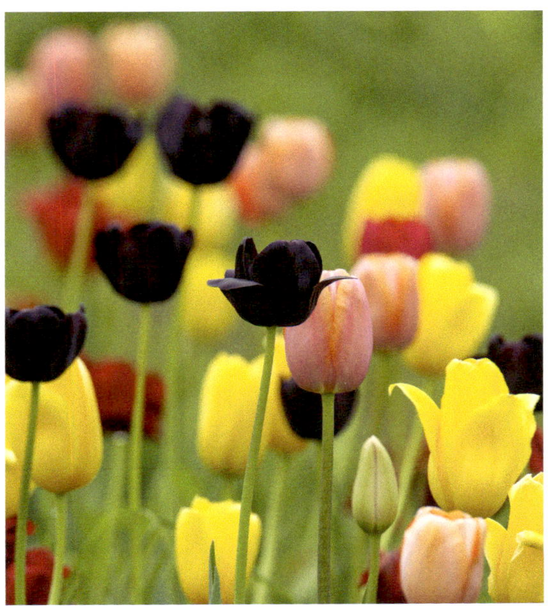

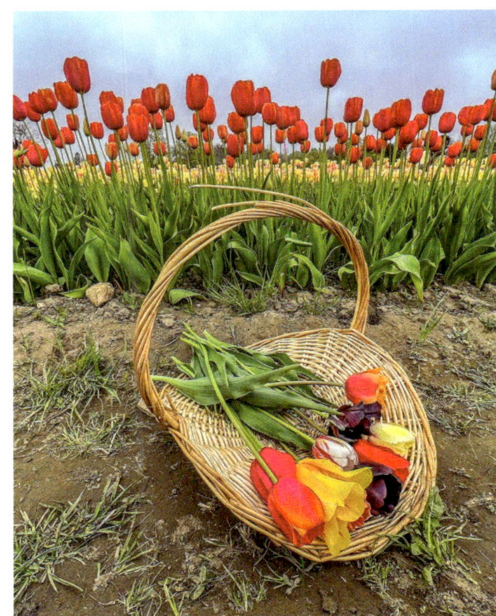

3

Hale Farm, Colebrook

Managed by the Colebrook Land Conservancy Organization, Hale Farm is the "Gateway to Colebrook." The barn dates back to 1797. The farmland is comprised of thirty-eight acres and is considered open space.

The Hale Barn sits at the crossroads of Stillman Hill Road and Rte. 183 in Colebrook. Stillman Hill Road, portioned as part of the Old North Road, was used for moving military troops and prisoners during the French and Indian War and the Revolutionary War.

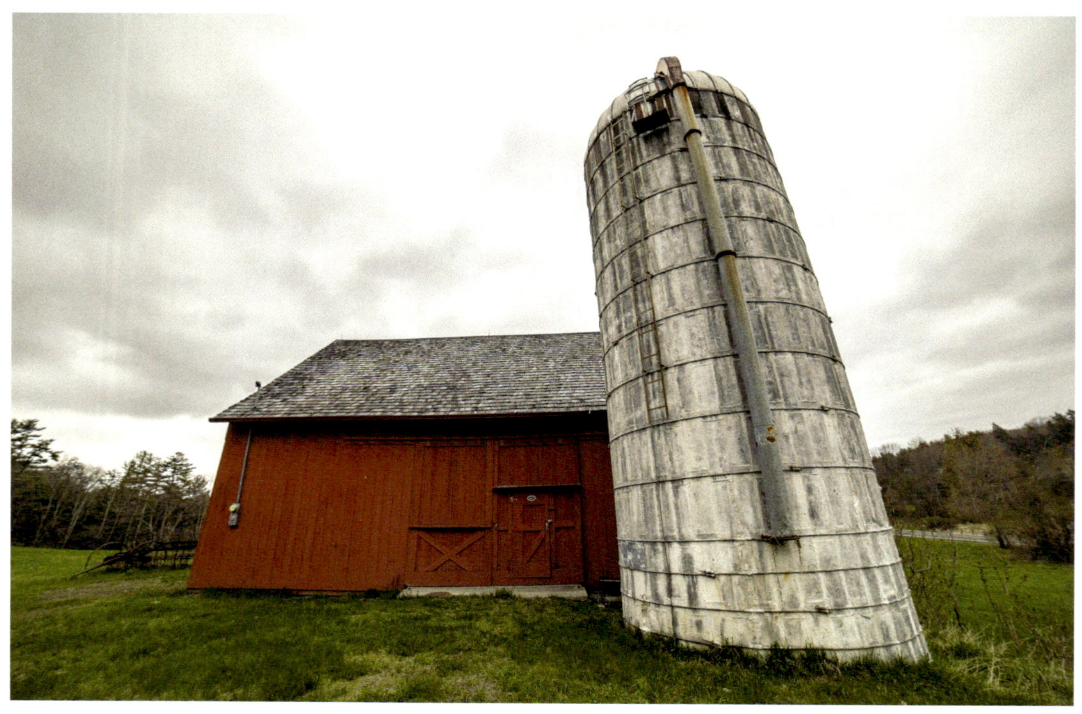

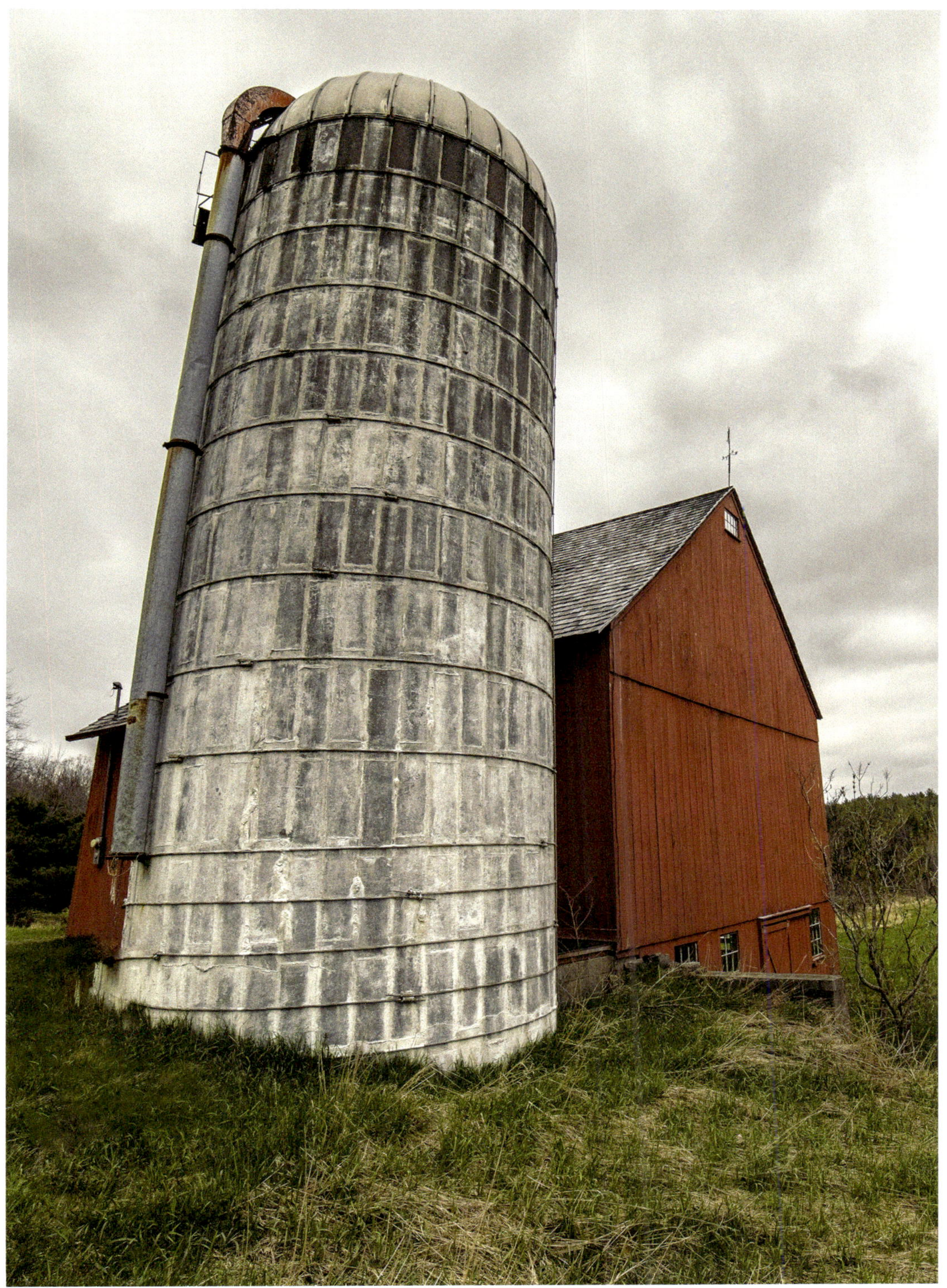

4
Chester Barns

Route 148 in Chester, CT, divides the land of an old saltbox barn now used to house horses. Chester remains one of the more artsy towns in Connecticut, offering hole-in-the-wall, farm-to-table restaurants and a booming farmer's market during spring and summer. This market provides your primary vegetable varieties, hard-to-find fruit like Black Currants, and a medley of mushrooms, cheeses, and artisan loaves of bread.

A corn crib barn frames a star from the town's Starry Night Illumination Celebration. The stars, made by a local artist, Christopher Owen, have exploded into over 150 stars throughout the city, illuminating winter's dark, cold nights. The primitive forms of Owen's stars accentuate the old-time feel of the town's many antique structures.

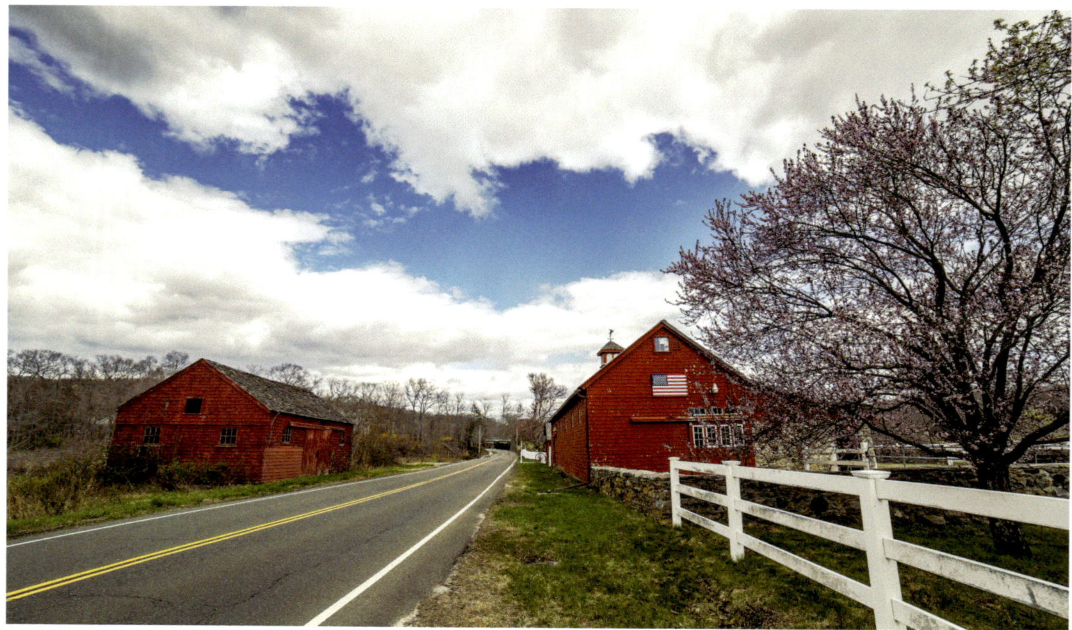

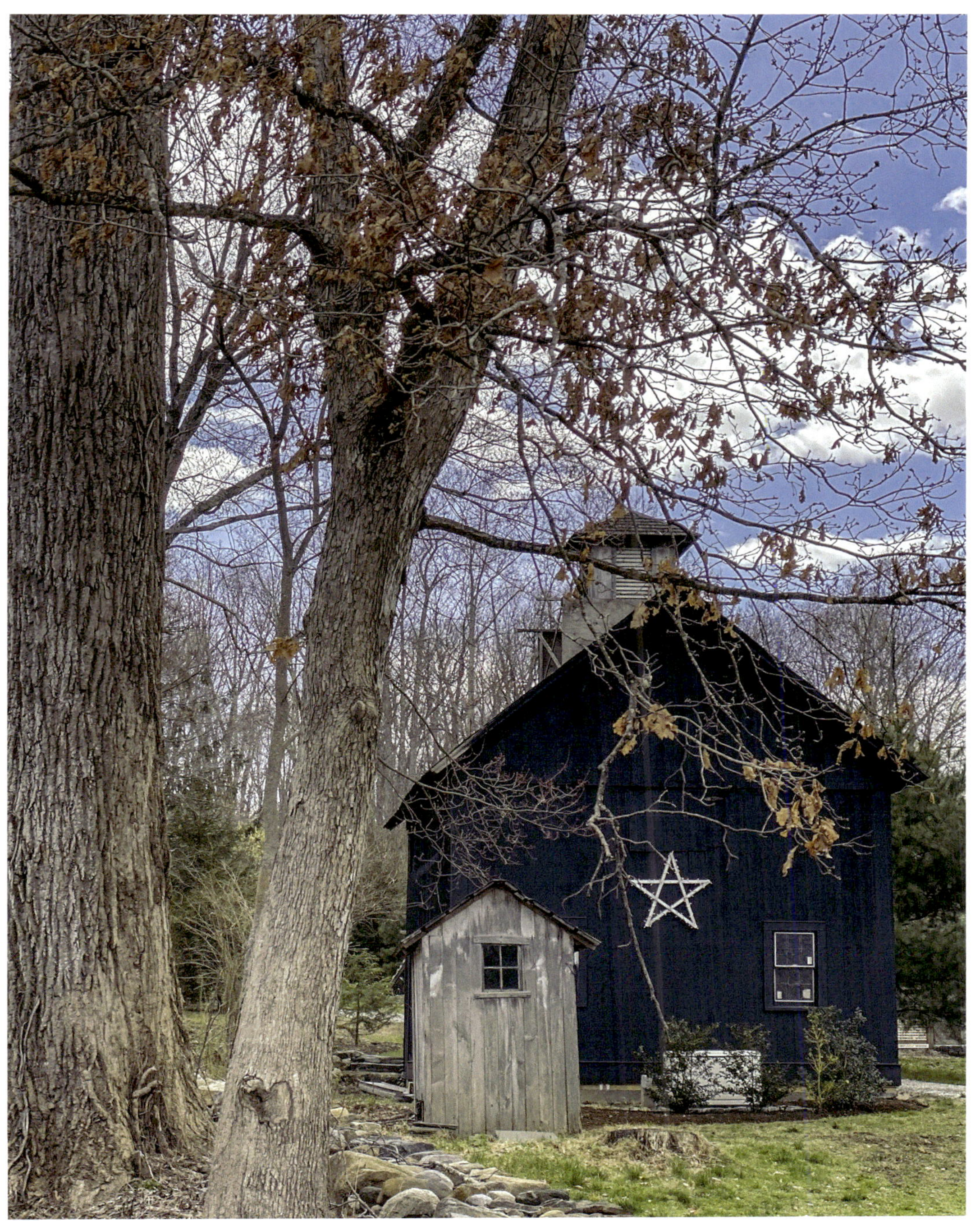

Preston Barns

Preston, a town in New London County, is also home to many old architectural gems, from asylums to historic barns. This barn epitomizes the red ochre hue that New England farmers painted their structures. The varnish applied to the barns was a mixture of linseed oil, lime, and iron oxide when exposed to the sun, transforming into the classic color of today.

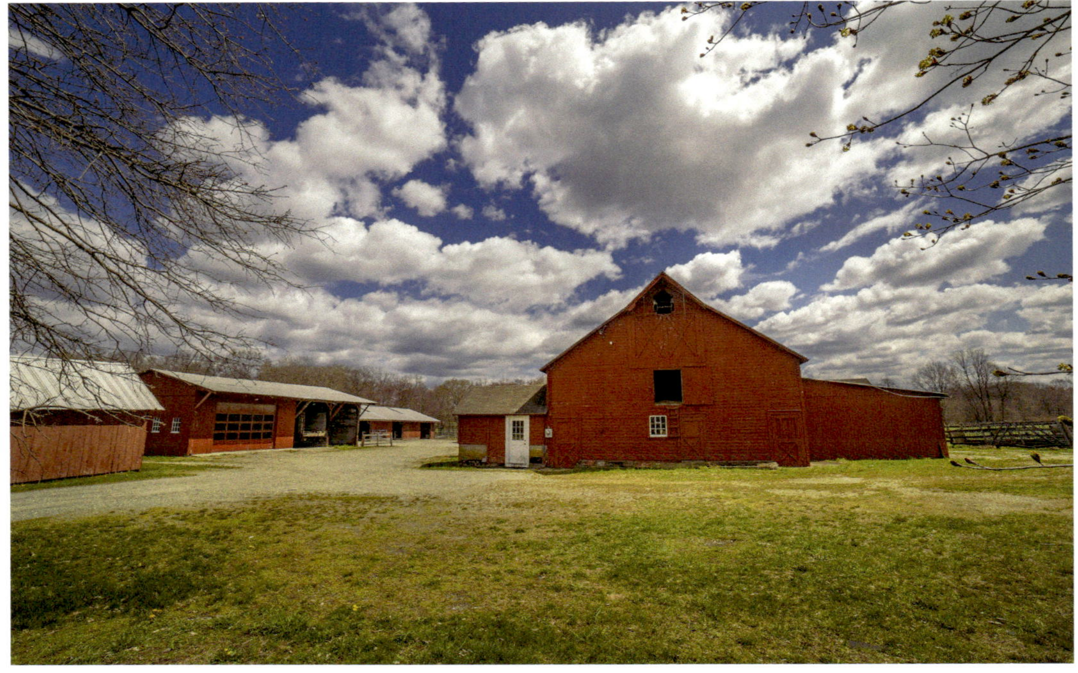

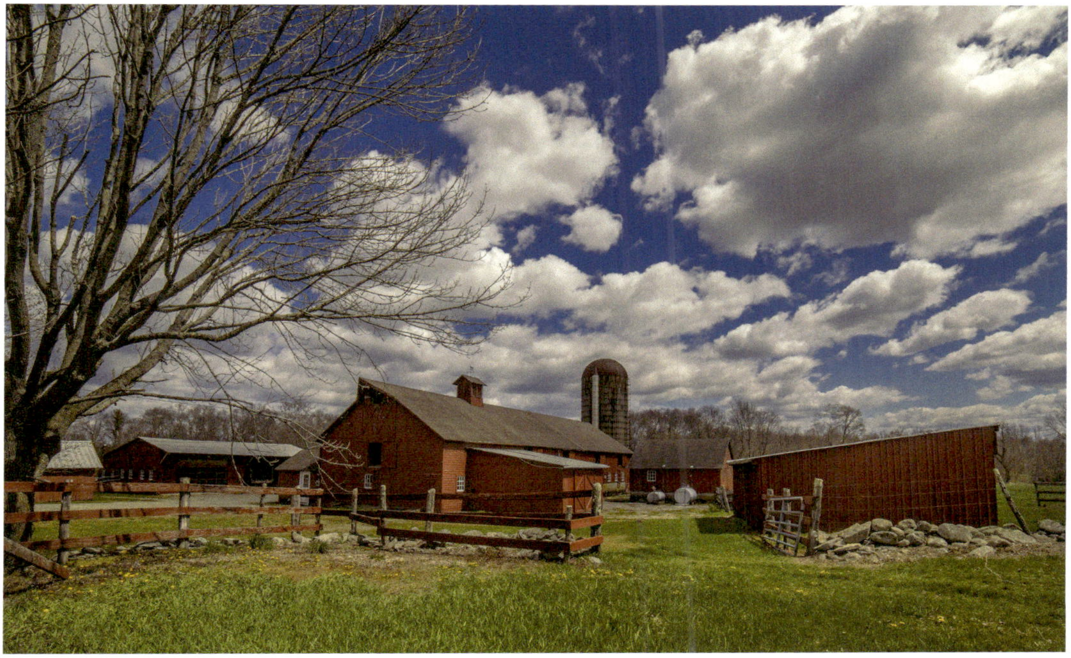

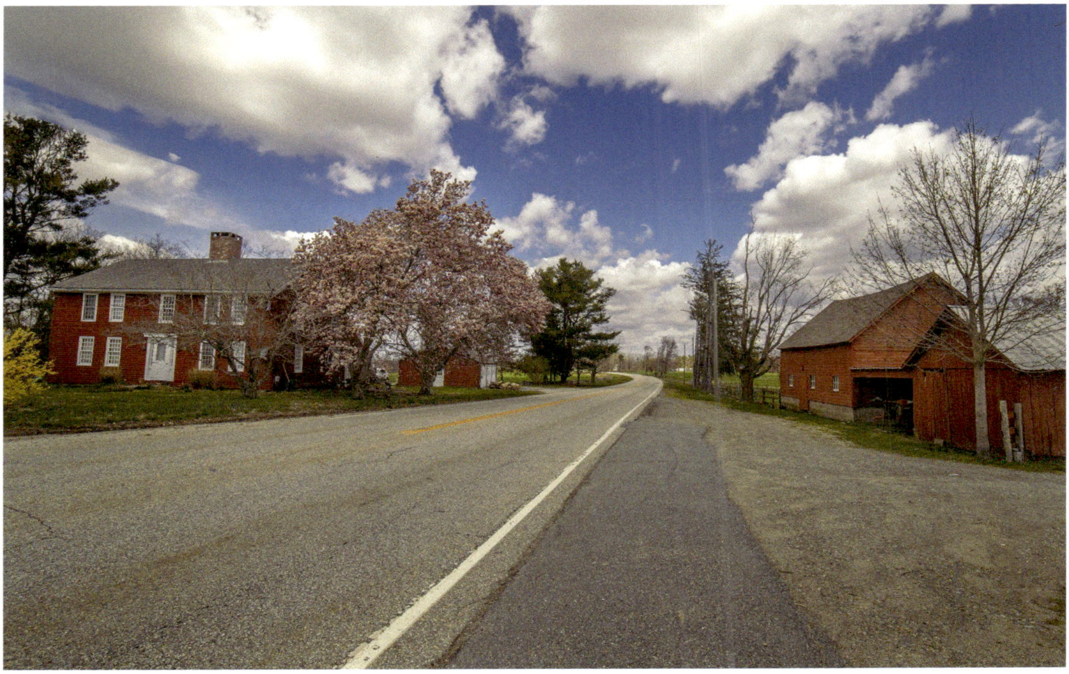

A beautifully crumbling gambrel barn and abandoned well, also known as Ayer Farm, decorates the roadside of Route 164 in Preston. At first glance, one would think this was a prairie barn. Prairie barns are easily distinguishable against the landscapes due to their peak overhang above the hay loft. Hay hoods are prominent features that closely resemble historic Dutch barns. However, engineers were developing new approaches to their dairy barns by the twentieth century to reduce the spread of tuberculosis by improving ventilation, hence the balloon-like gambrel tongue in groove roof. The space above still embodies a place for hay while keeping the manure and airborne dust to a minimum while implementing concrete floors and manure basements.

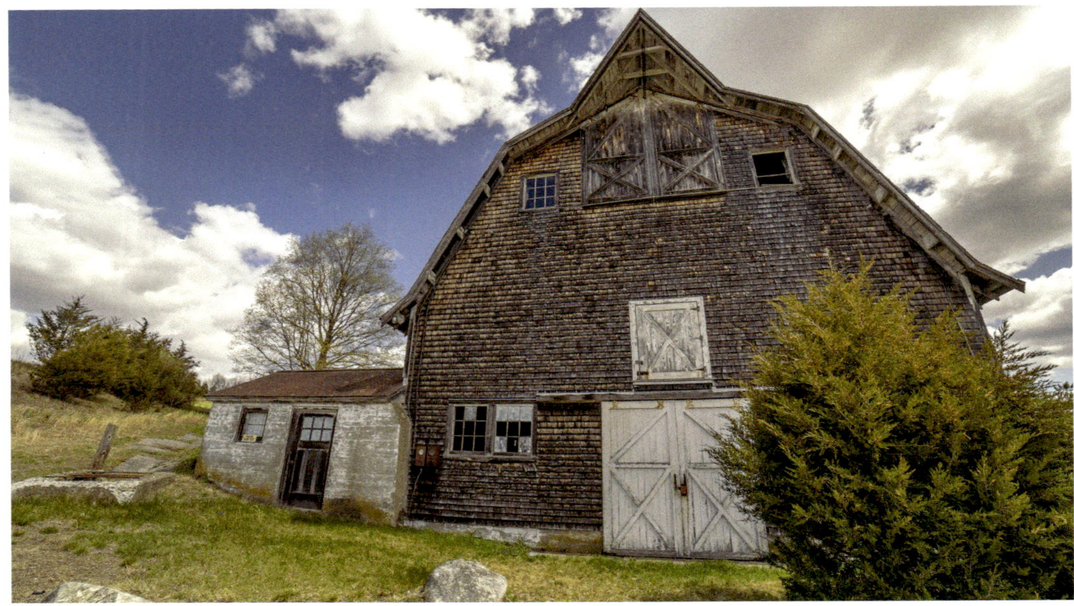

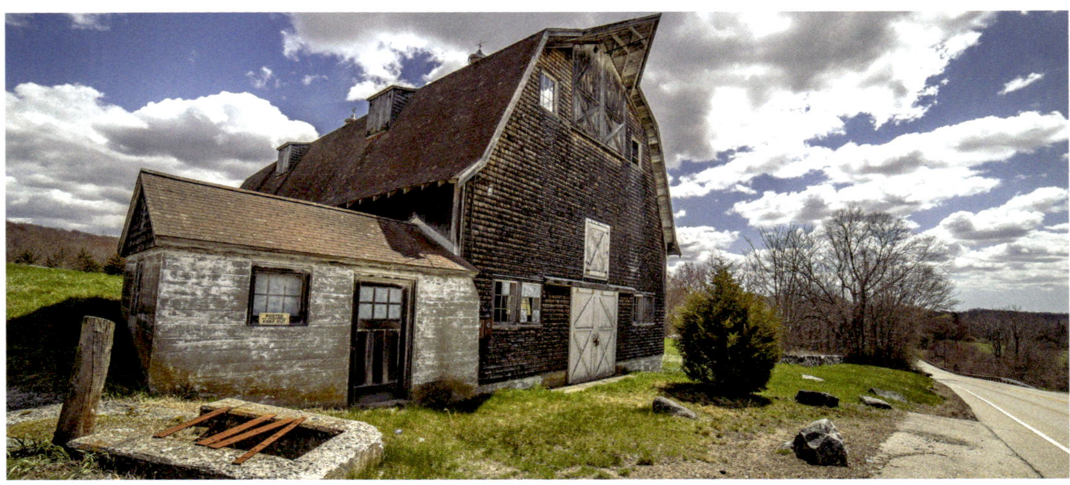

Southbury, Roxbury, Shelton Areas

Southbury

The barns at Southbury Training School are mostly abandoned but occasionally leased out to farmers in the town for their cattle, to graze, seek shelter, and for the residents to store their equipment. Initially, the school's farms were conceived to provide patients and housed employees with fresh food from a self-sustaining community. The Wisconsin-style dairy barns also share the property with chicken coops, ground-level stables, butcher sheds, and wagon sheds with various roof types like gable, gambrel, and hip.

A corn crib barn in classic New England red sits at a dirt road entrance and Cassidy Road in Southbury. This Christmas tree farm also has a large English A-frame barn to the back of the property. Listed only as the Southbury Training School Poultry and Christmas Tree Farm, no one would know otherwise that it was a part of the training school. People flock here during the holiday season for fresh Christmas trees. During spring and summer, it is a local hotspot for birding and wildlife. At any given time, groups of bluebirds, harriers, eagles, kestrels, droves of songbirds, and a family of bobcats are hunting the surrounding fields.

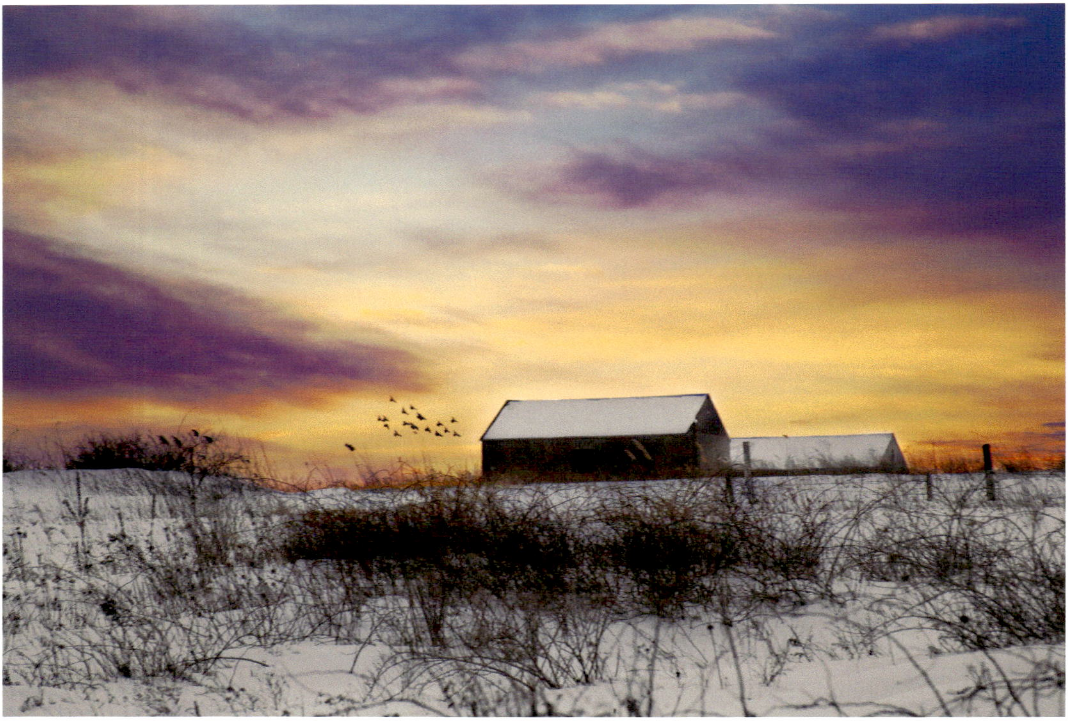

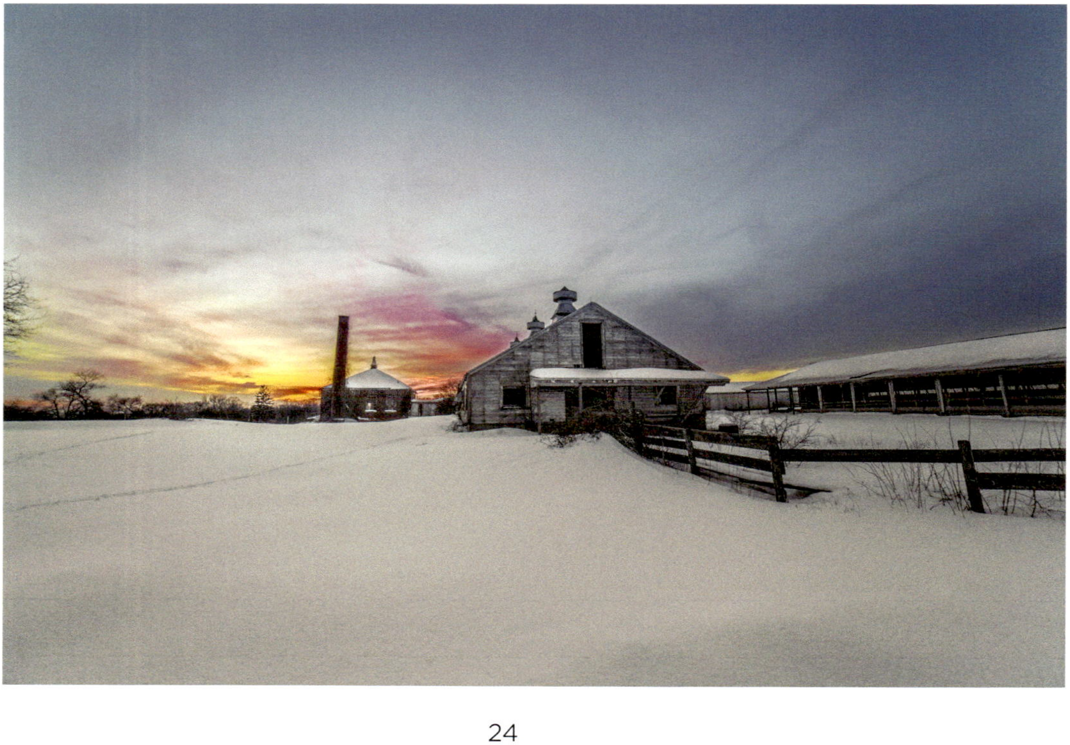

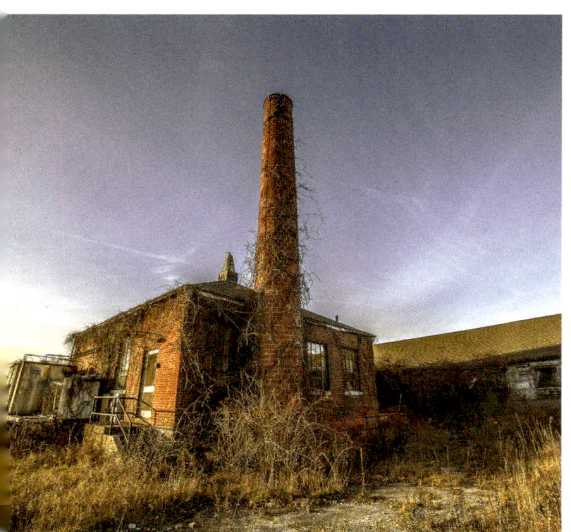
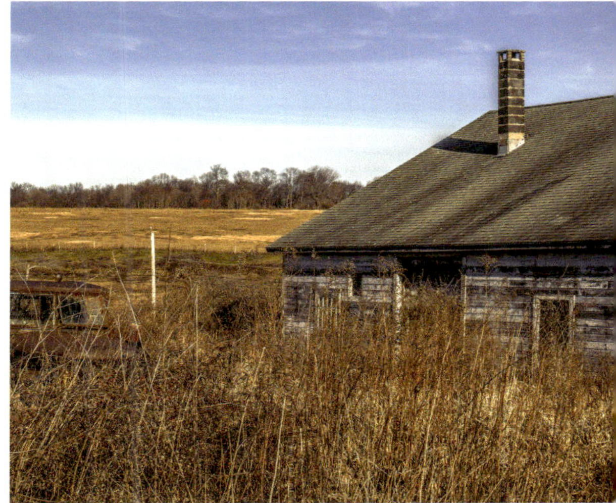

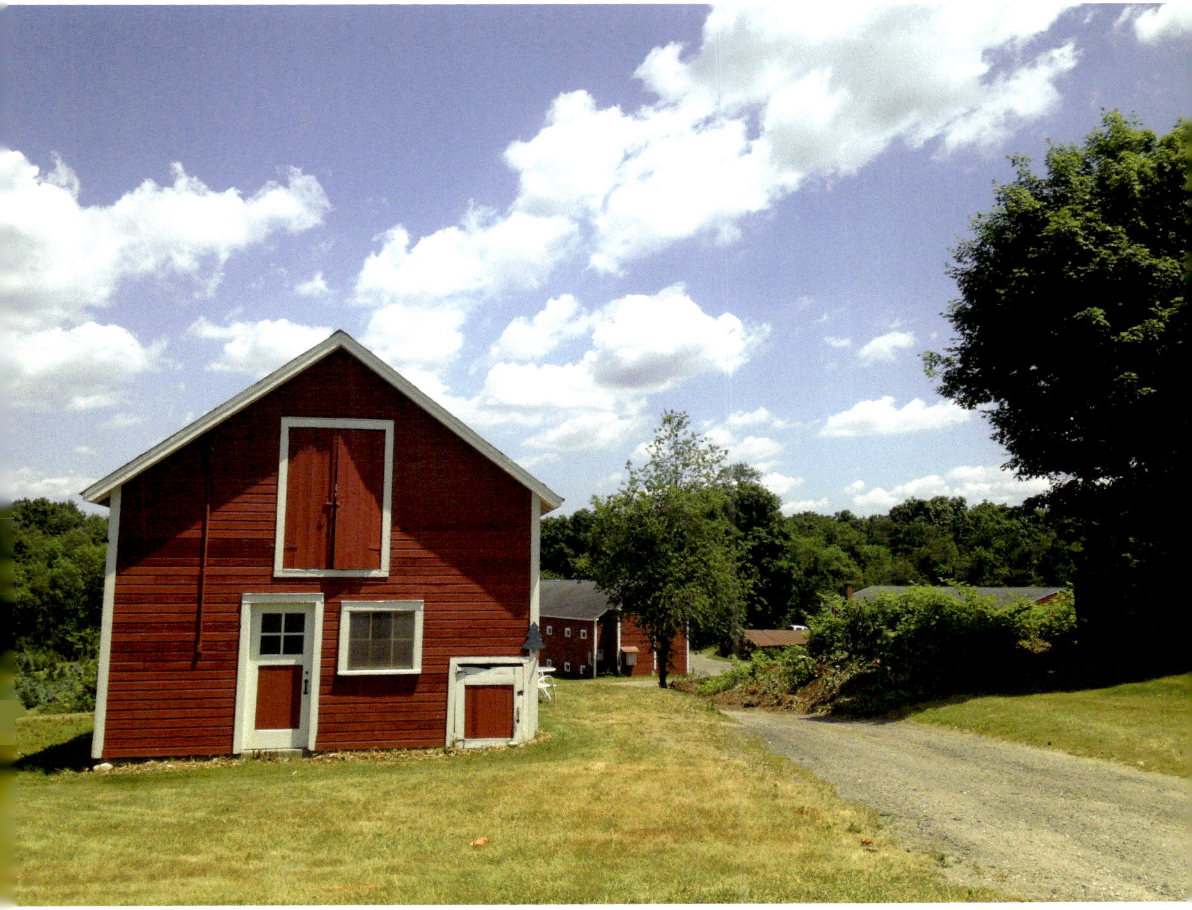

Roxbury

An old, collapsing homestead with a pitched roof and ferrous oxide red barn sits atop a high point in Roxbury, CT. It is easy to get lost in the area's scenic beauty, especially in the fall, with colors as far as one can see. The New England red barn color was also said to have animal blood mixed in the linseed oil to get the red-orange color. Mixing the protective coat provided another benefit and was told to prevent the growth of fungi and mold.

A patriotic English bank barn named Greyledge Farm sits against the autumn backdrop of the Roxbury hills. Built in 1939, the farm has remained in the Fitzgerald family since the early nineties. Here, the Fitzgeralds began raising Black Angus cattle to feed their family and residents' locavore tastes. Locavores eat only within the local food supply, grown or raised in the immediate area. The fieldstone base and well-kept vertical and clapboard siding make this barn a highly photographed structure within the Connecticut landscape.

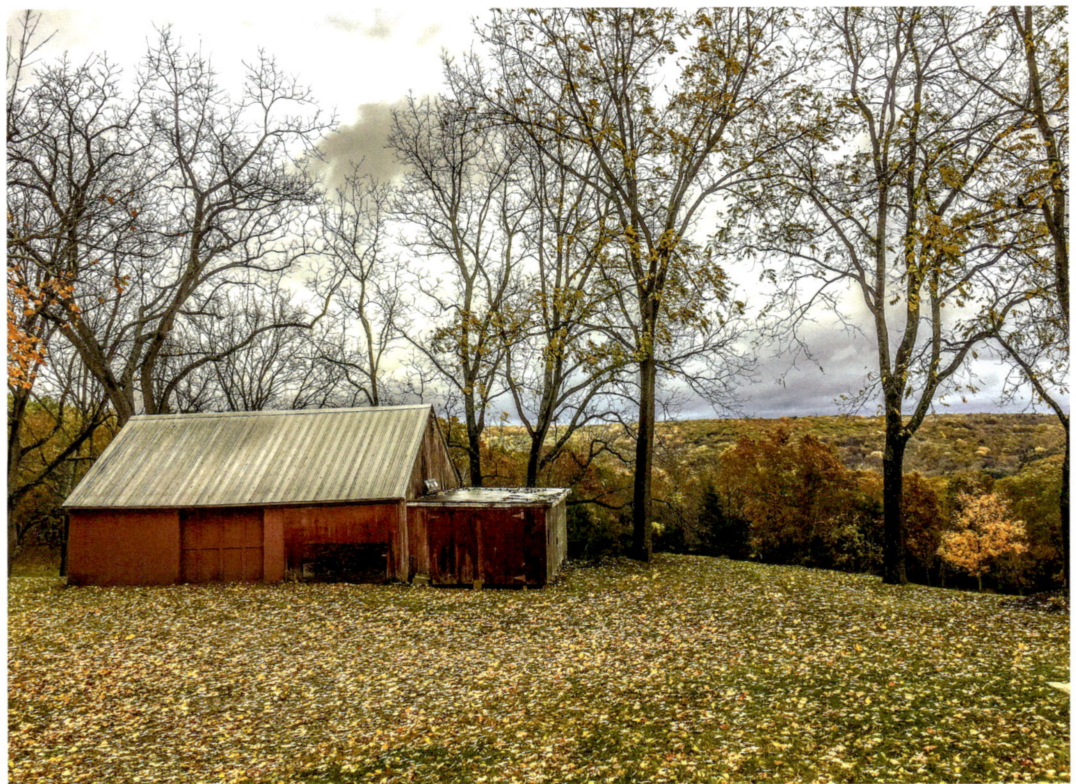

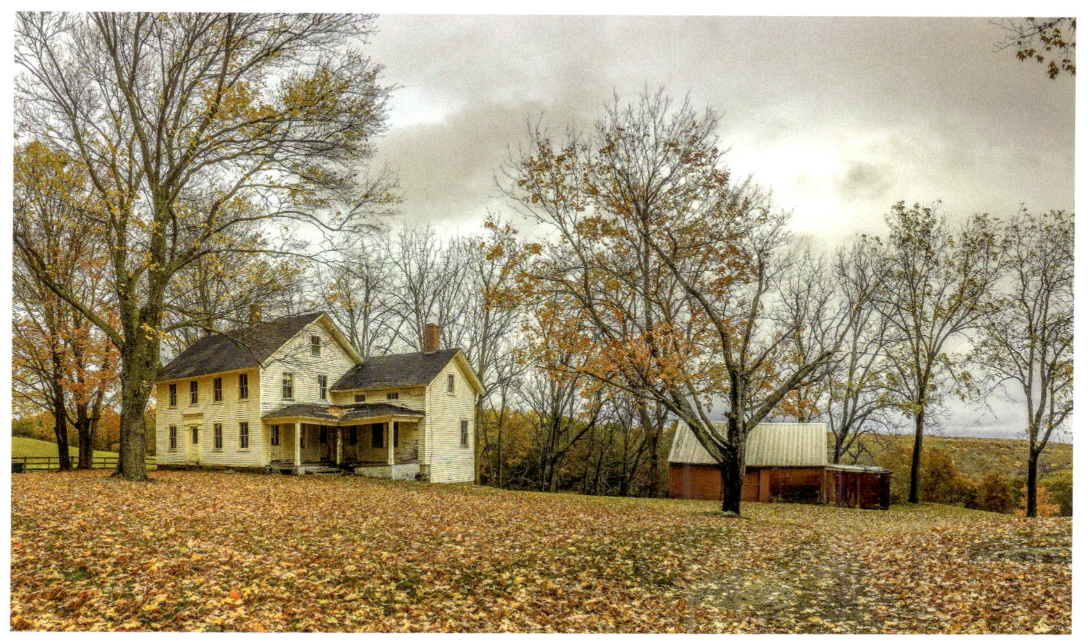

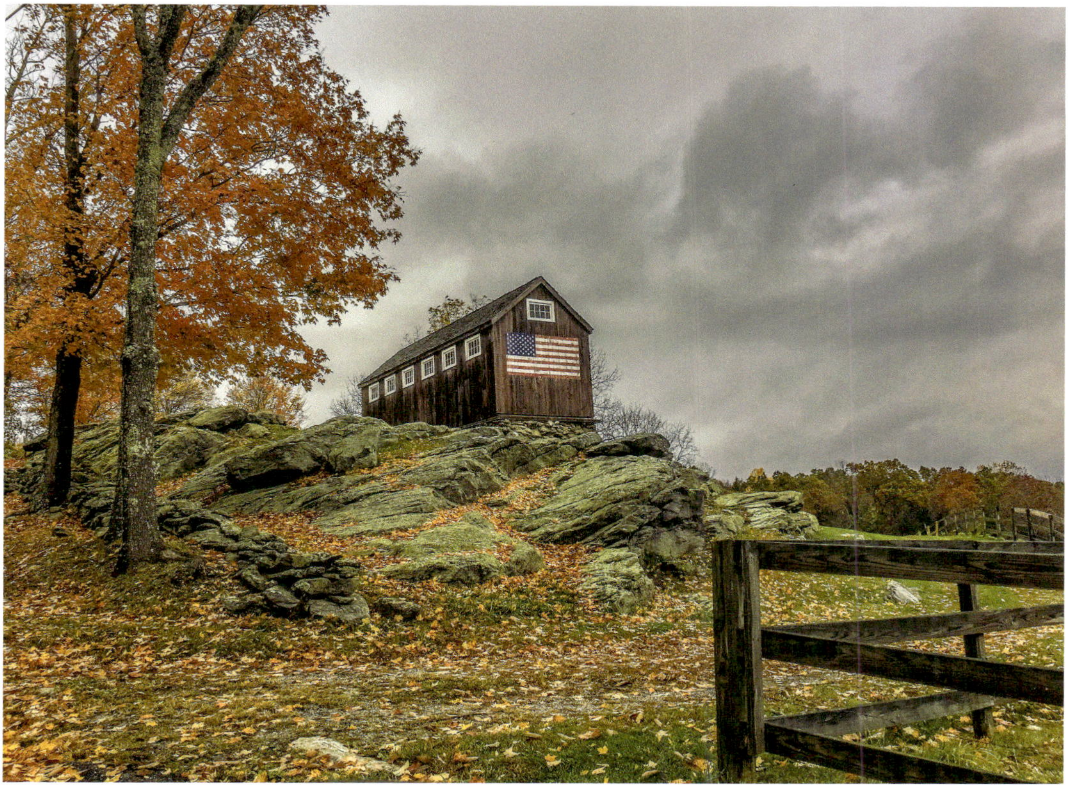

Shelton

A Shelton, CT English/New England hybrid/bank and gambrel barn, farmhouse, and silo is viewed through the golden leaves of fall. Situated off Birdseye Road, this farm has views of Long Island. The Connecticut Barn Organization reports that this may be one of the few reverse assembly frames used in a barn in Connecticut.

Redding

The Superman Barn, Redding, CT is located in Fairfield County. Fairfield County is #8 in Connecticut with the most farms. Eighteen farms reside in Fairfield County as of June 2023. This Redding Barn, dubbed The Superman Barn, is home to artist Don Messer. Don works in ceramics, wood, metal, and paint. I took this photo in passing, running across Connecticut, snapping everything I saw, and wishing I remembered where I had taken it. I was so enamored with it that it was the only image of my own that I hung in our home. I looked at it every day and wished I had remembered where I took it to revisit it. At the end of this book, I finally found out what town and what it was precisely, thanks to Preservation Connecticut and a Facebook post they made for me. I want to express to Don Messer the sheer happiness his home and studio have brought me every day for eight years on my wall until I moved to Maine.

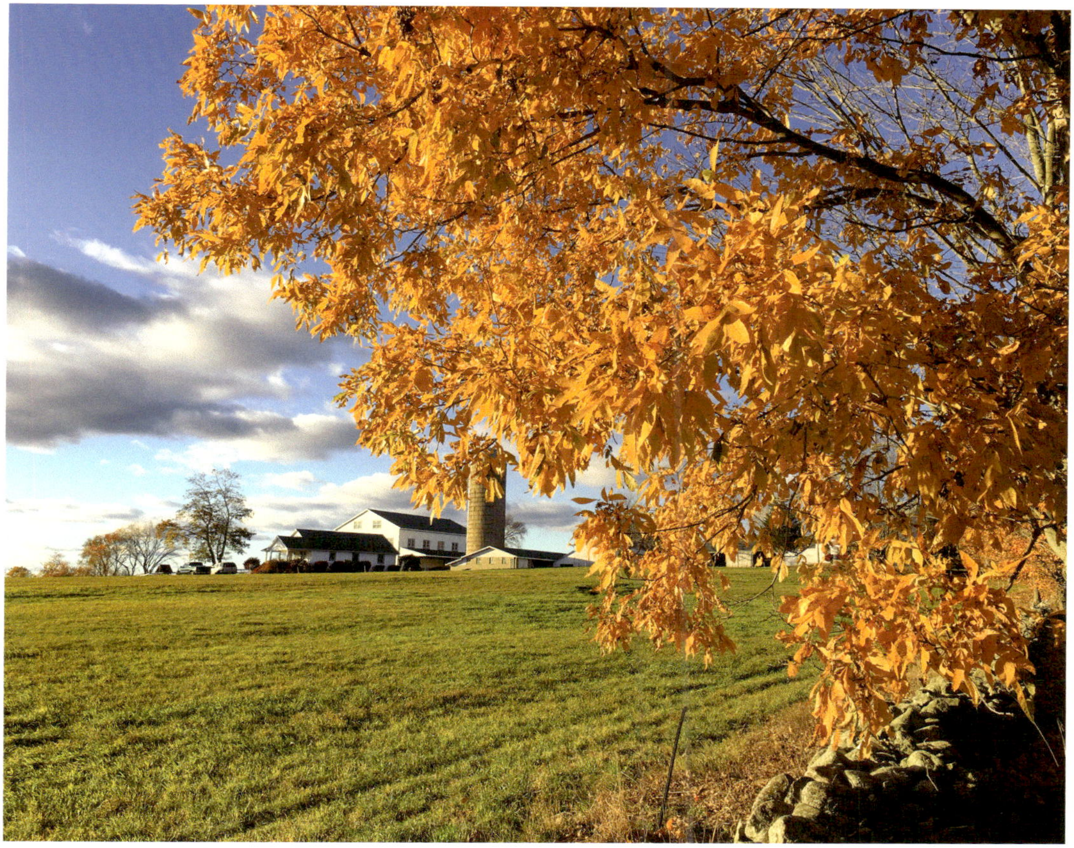

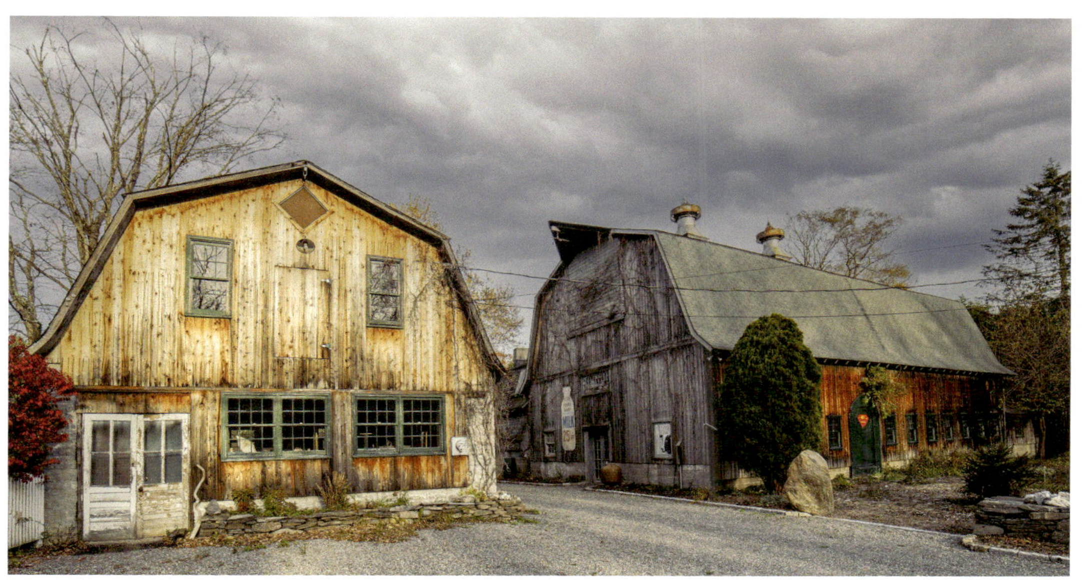

Newtown

This barn from Newtown, CT, was owned by the Roman Catholic Diocese of Bridgeport until sold to pay off settlements in their sexual abuse lawsuits. The shelter was the last standing structure before suspected arsonists burned the property to the ground. Special features boasted a full, entertaining kitchen and roomy living space. The property was initially owned by the Gretsch family from Gretsch Guitars. It was often called the Jewel or Crown of Castle Hill because of the sprawling mansion next to the barn.

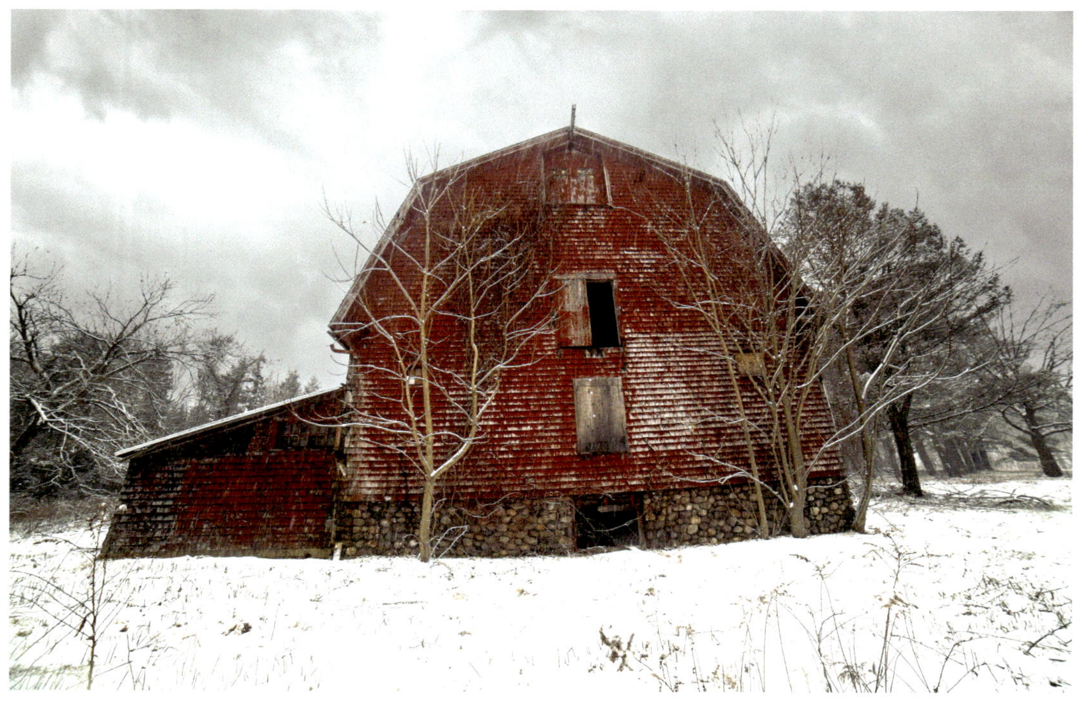

8
Enfield Tobacco Barns

Coming from North Carolina, I understand the sticky, pungent, and hard work of picking flue-cured and Burley Tobacco. However, I needed to be more knowledgeable about the crop's abundance in Connecticut until I saw the staggering bones of their marvelous tobacco barns. The crop even has its own Connecticut shade-grown version. Cultivated in the shade, away from direct sunlight, this monoculture is often prized for its elegant taste, subtle sweetness, and color. It is used chiefly for wrappers for cigars. Farmers will tell you it tastes like no other, and the soil in the valley contributes to the flavor. In addition to the Connecticut River Valley, Massachusetts is another grower of shade tobacco. Tobacco was a big business in Enfield and the Connecticut River Valley, and until you see the 200–300-foot barns in rows, you cannot fathom how big they were. These gable structures tower over the winding roads that run through the town and mark the history of a crop that has sustained its farmers but trembles in the hands of modern society.

In the 1940s, Martin Luther King Jr. worked tobacco in Connecticut for three seasons. Dr. King worked the Simsbury, CT, barns, and it is rumored that his time working in this area spurred his life goals to go past the segregated South. Windsor's sheds were recently torn down to the outcry of many with a wish to preserve them. OJ Thrall, Inc., the original owners of the land for upwards of 373 years, sold the property to developers and are now trading their tobacco crops on their remaining land for barley, wheat, and various grains instead. Sadly, replacing the history of the razed barns is a $213 million sports and entertainment complex.

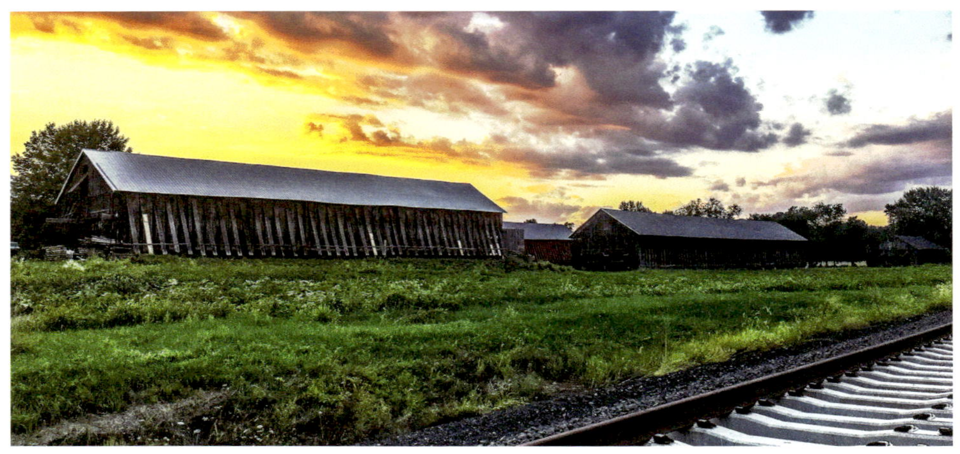

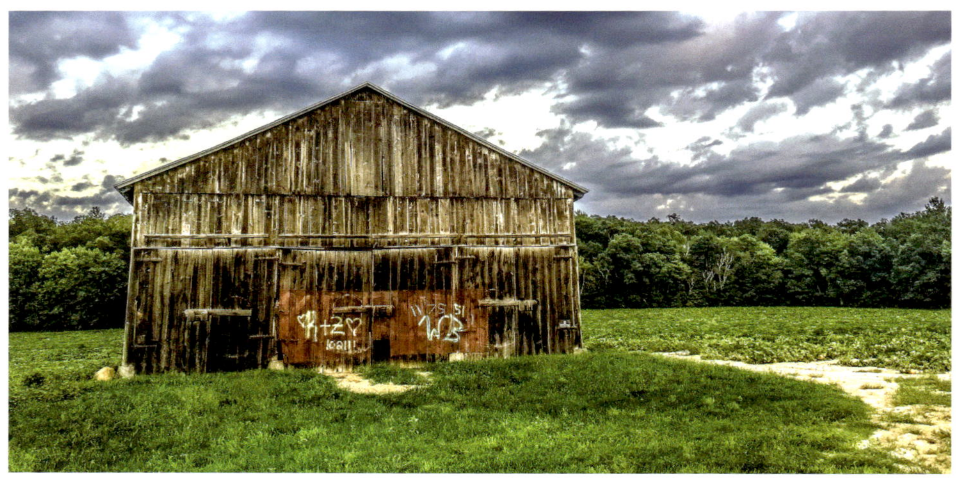

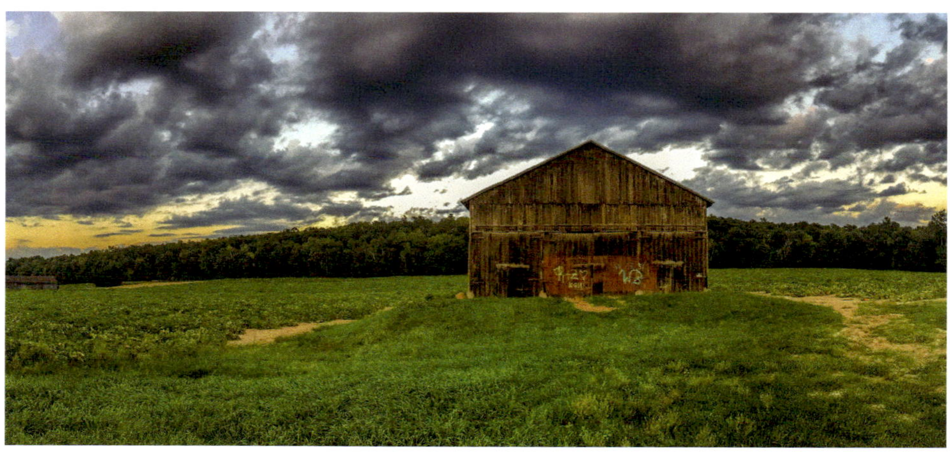

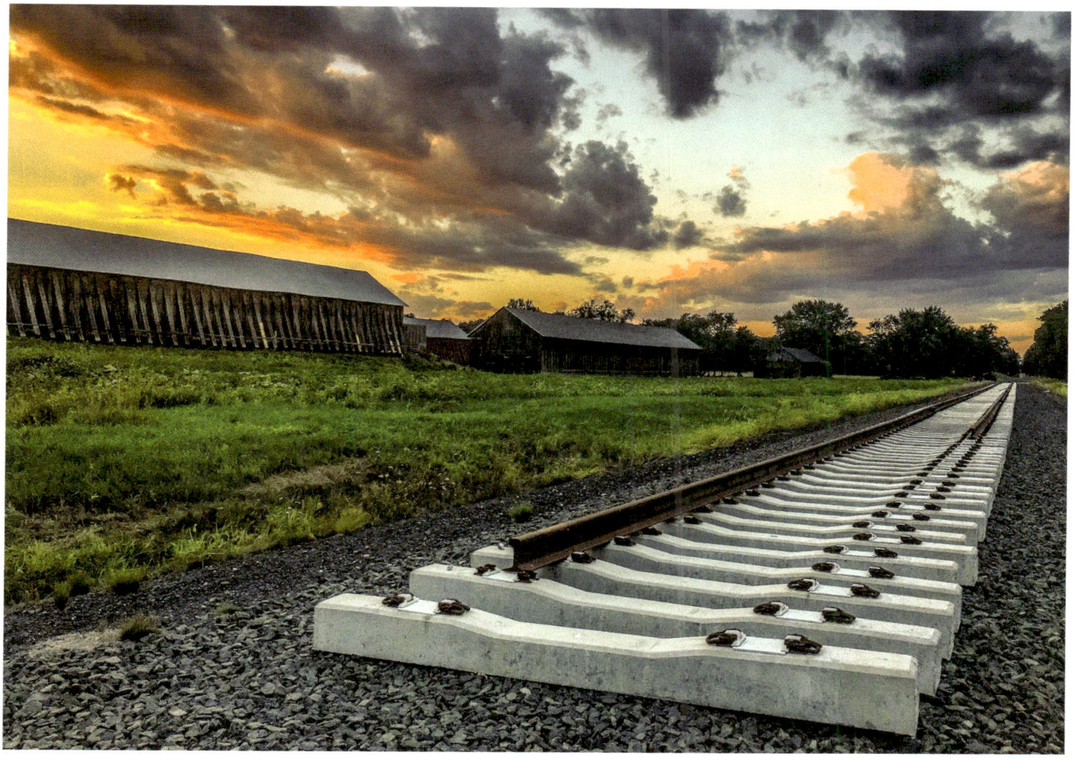

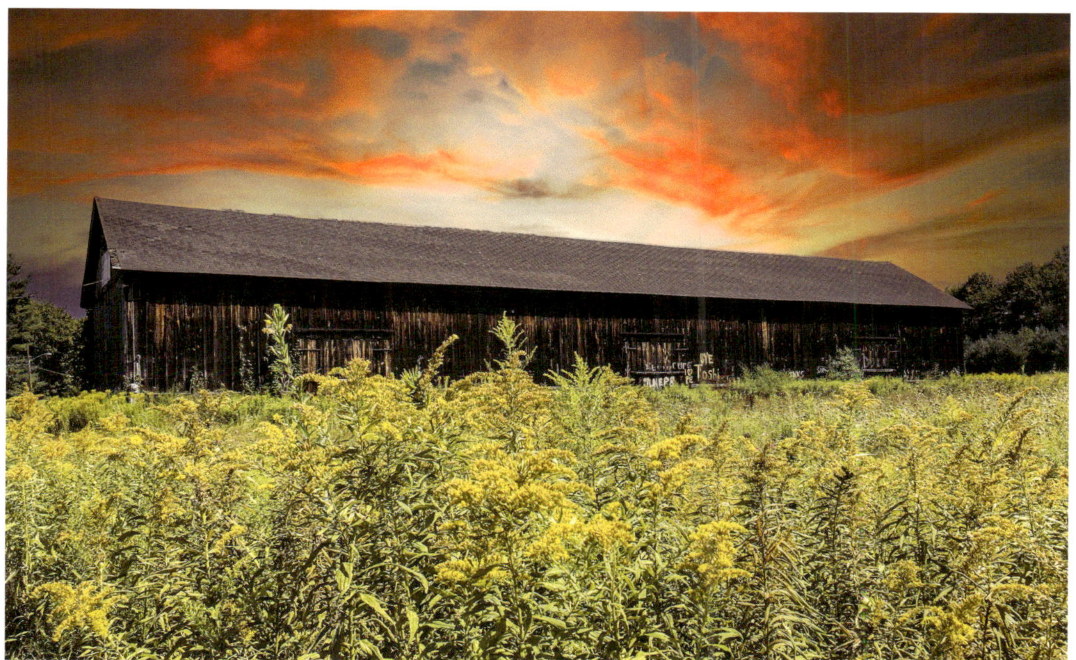

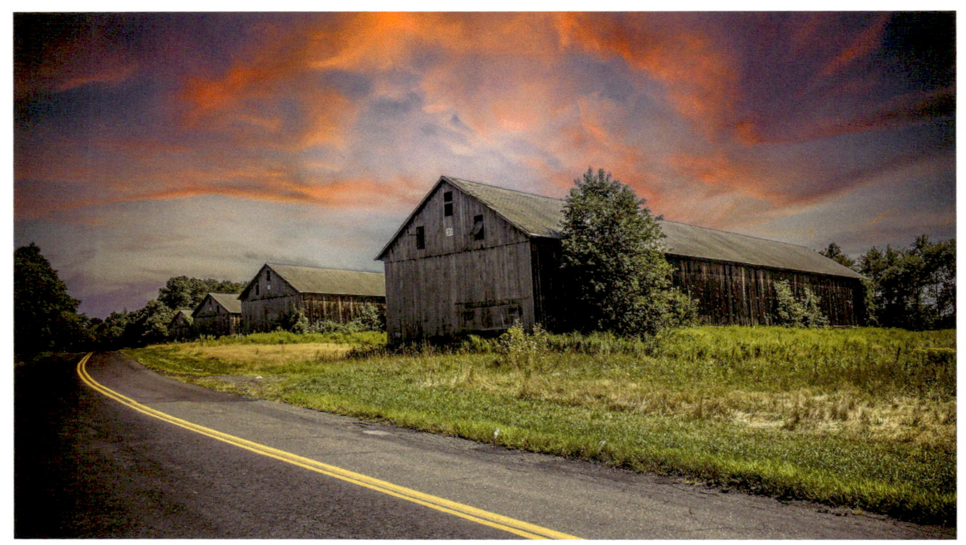

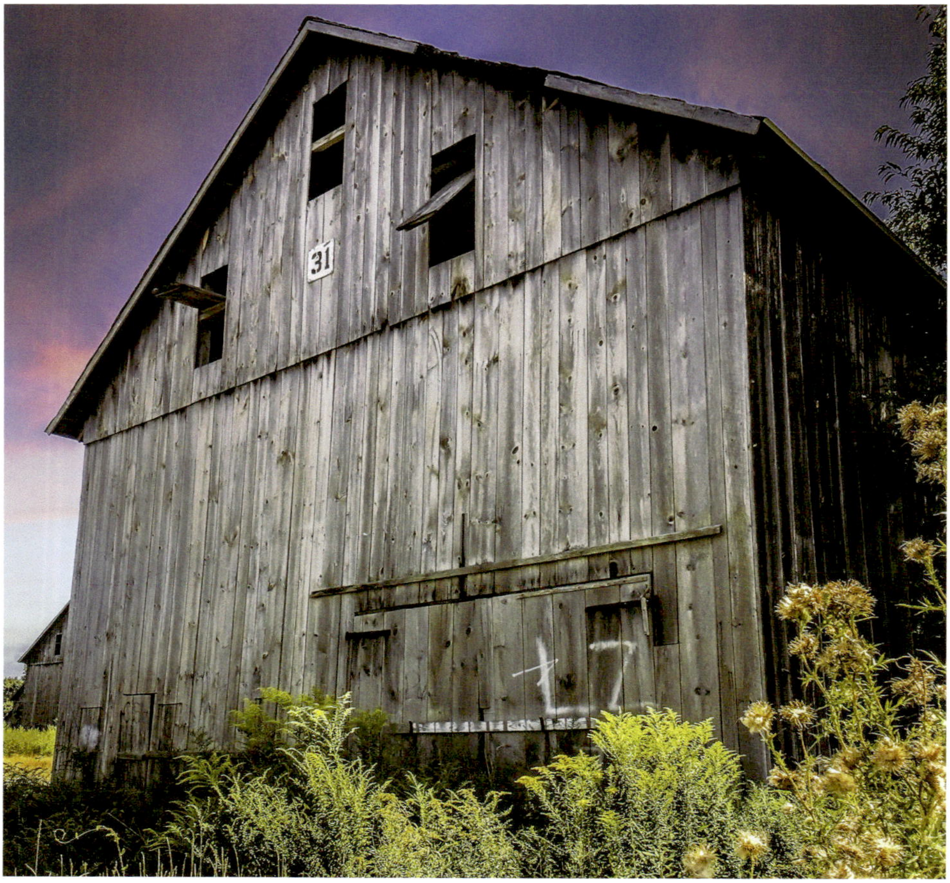

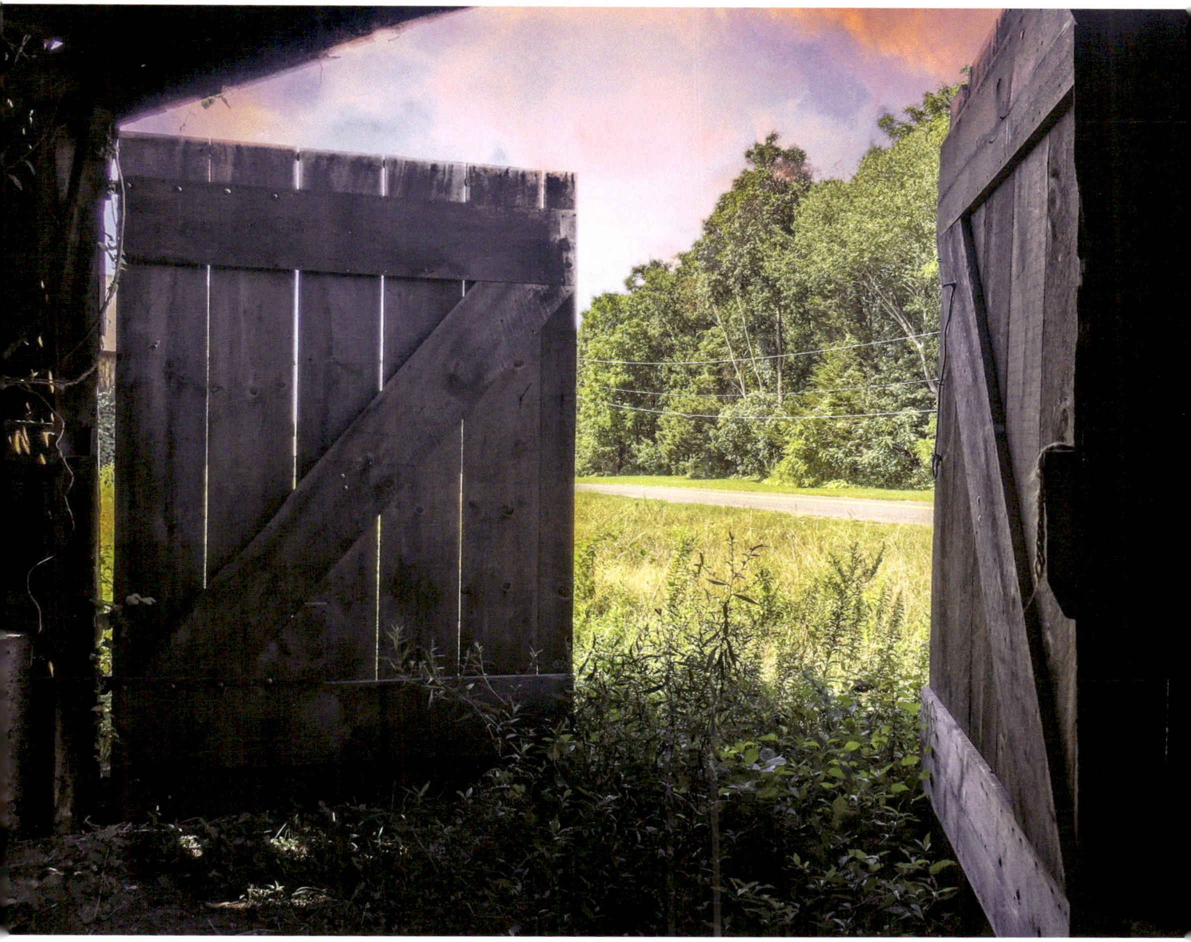

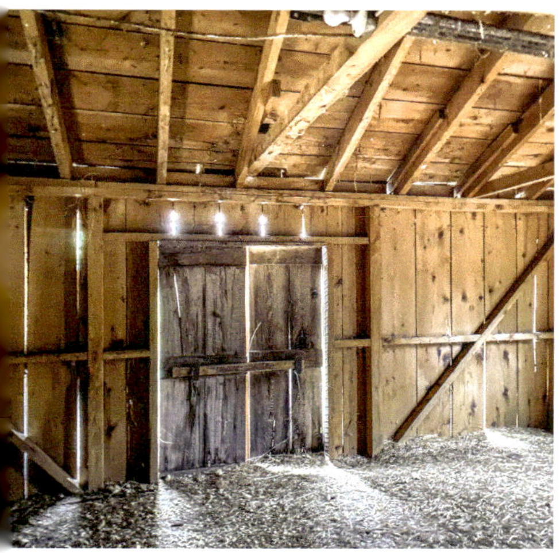

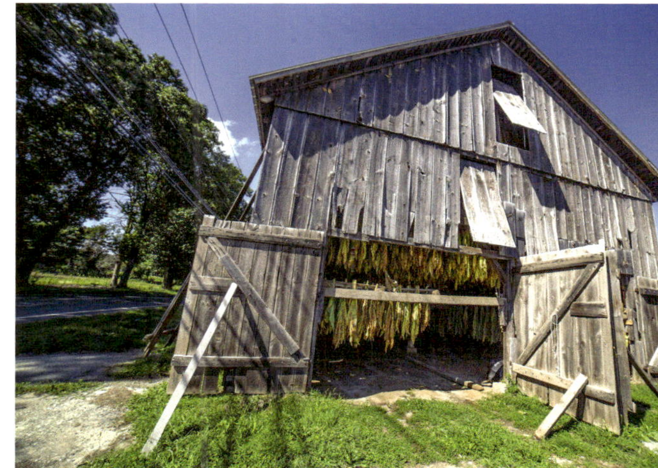

9
Orange

Prindle Hill Road in Orange, CT, is home to J. Latella and Sons Piggery. I remember calling one day to ask if they could help me, and my Southern accent must have relayed something very, very different, as the man on the phone asked me, "What do you want killed?" I had a moment where I had to think about this opportunity. I wanted to know what kind of dog they had on the property I had fallen in love with. A friendly, intelligent farm dog that was tough enough to chow down on some hedge clippers but followed me on my photographic escapades. I adored him, this spunky little blue healer.

Latellas was founded in 1896 and now has state-of-the-art processing for many livestock. Latellas also offers pig roasts and rentals for the roasts. However, I still have to explain pig pickin' to many people. Shown is one of the last, barely standing horse barns on the property.

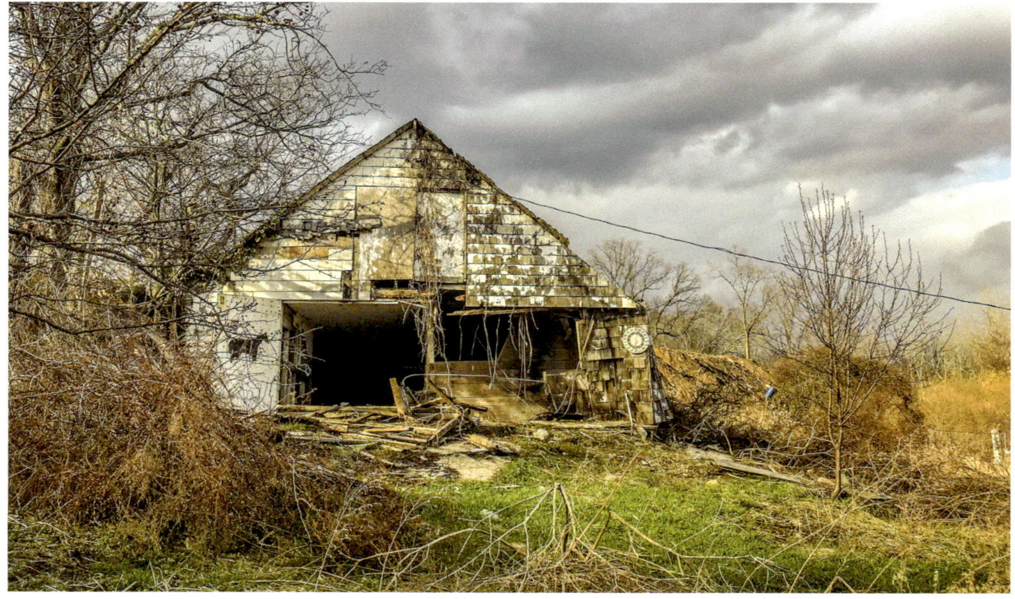

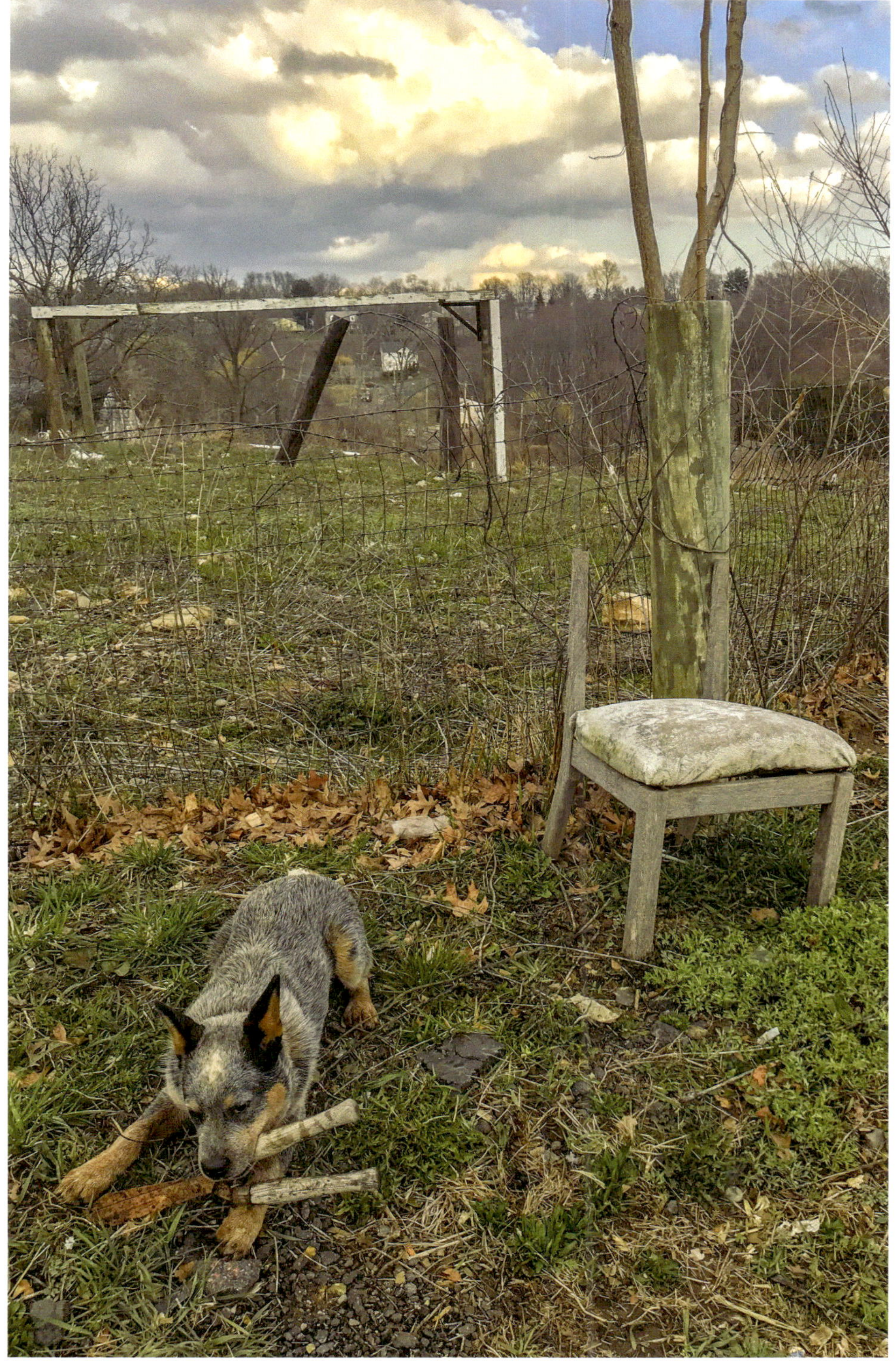

10

Killingworth, Clinton, Durham, and Madison

Killingworth

Killingworth is an untouched nook of Connecticut. Quaint farms accent the winding roads through lush green woodland. Barns often look as if time stood still. The town hosts a yearly Farm Day, where the local farmers invite people to come and visit a working farm while learning about what they do. This Dutch hybrid barn sits across from a vast cranberry bog. Killingworth also has an open farm day for residents to go down into the bogs and pick as many cranberries as they like.

David Graham and Killingworth residents pick cranberries for Thanksgiving in one of the many public land cranberry bogs. Antique coffee cans on rope are handed out to participants to collect their berries. The cranberries tumble into a large Ziplock provided by volunteers and are then ready to be taken home. There is never a limit to how much you can collect.

My muse was the hex mark and board barn on the property, where I spent some of the best days of my life. Since 2017, I have seen this barn twice daily, going to work and coming home, sometimes more during our walks. It was lovely in the winter, spring, summer, and fall with its ever-changing face. It housed drying bamboo and a sleigh made by a master artist from upstate New York. The sleigh pictured is a gift to the property's owner. They used the sleigh for many Christmas charitable events and to distribute presents to their employees' children. Now it rests below a dank, damp, caving roof, as it is just a matter of time before its vibrant seats are wearing rotten barn wood and raccoon poop. In 2023, I lost my significant other and had to say goodbye to the barn, critters, and property I had lived in and loved for seven years.

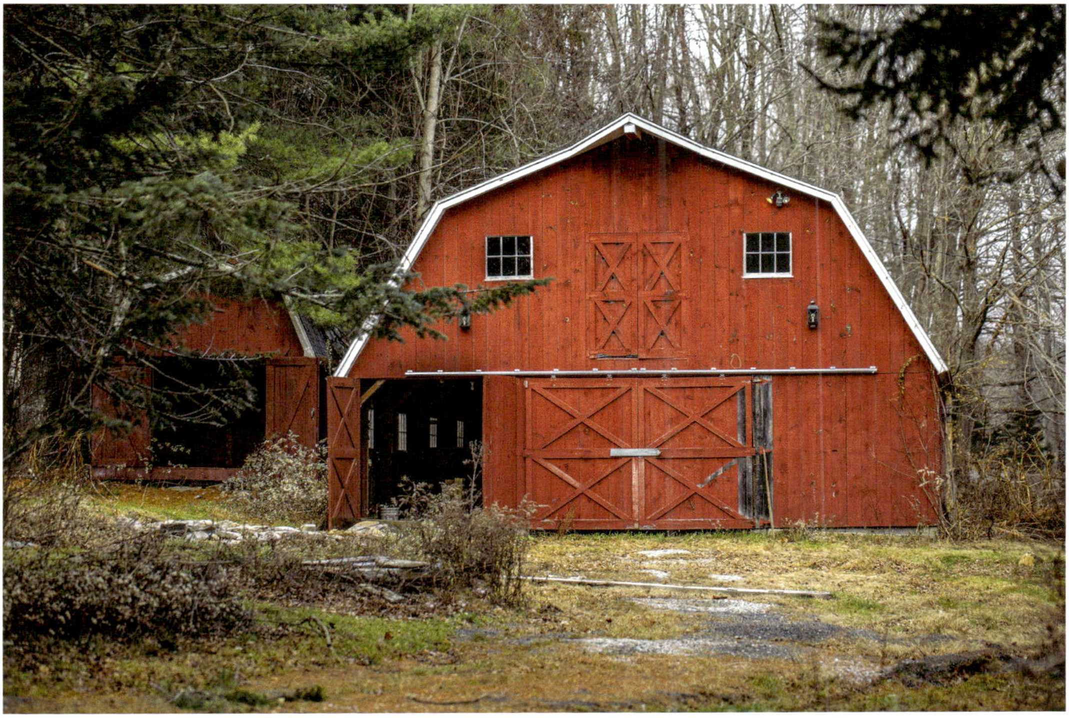

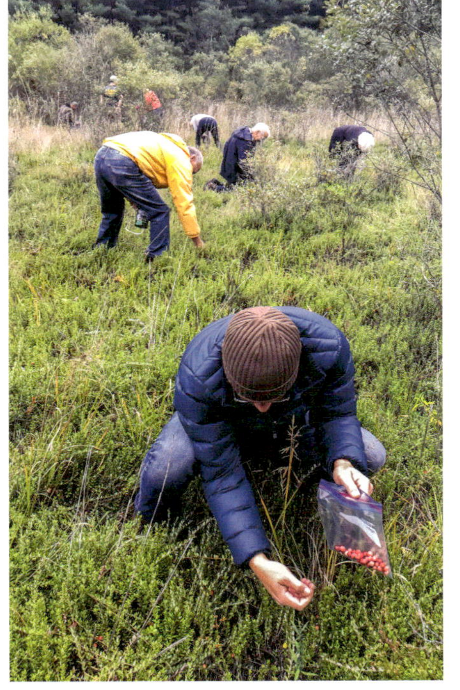

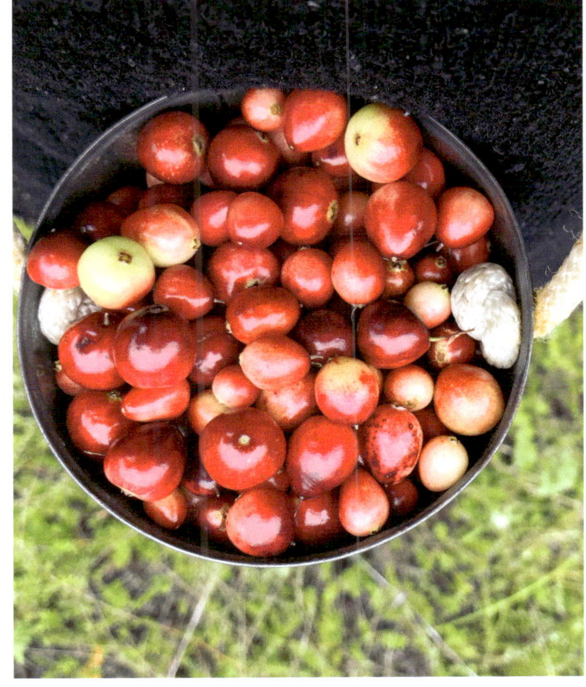

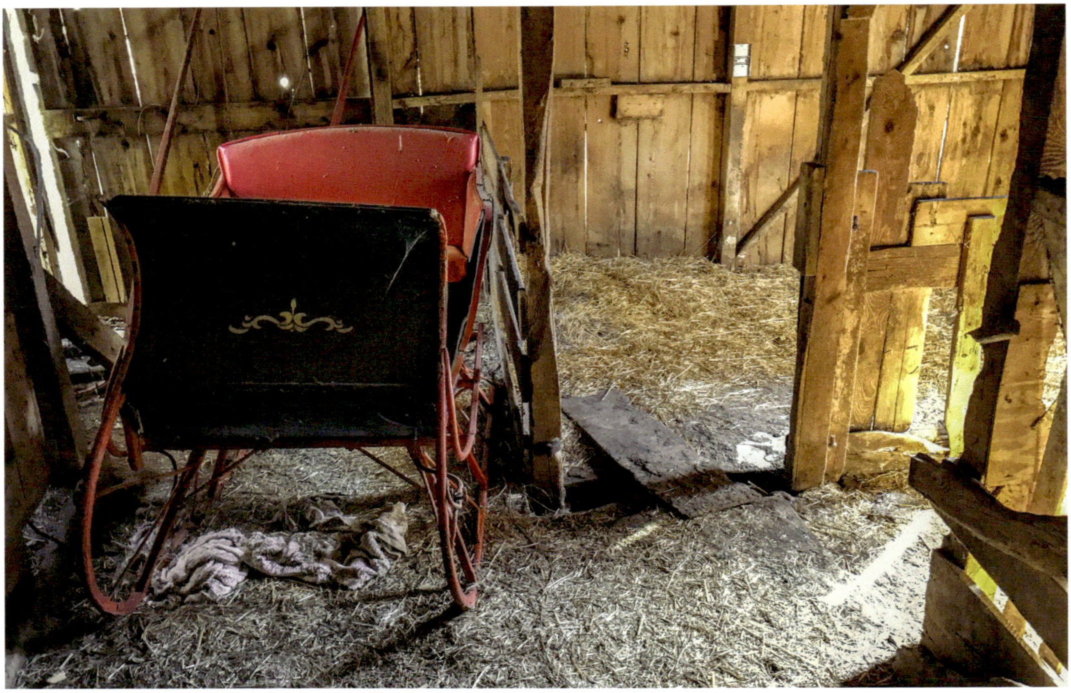

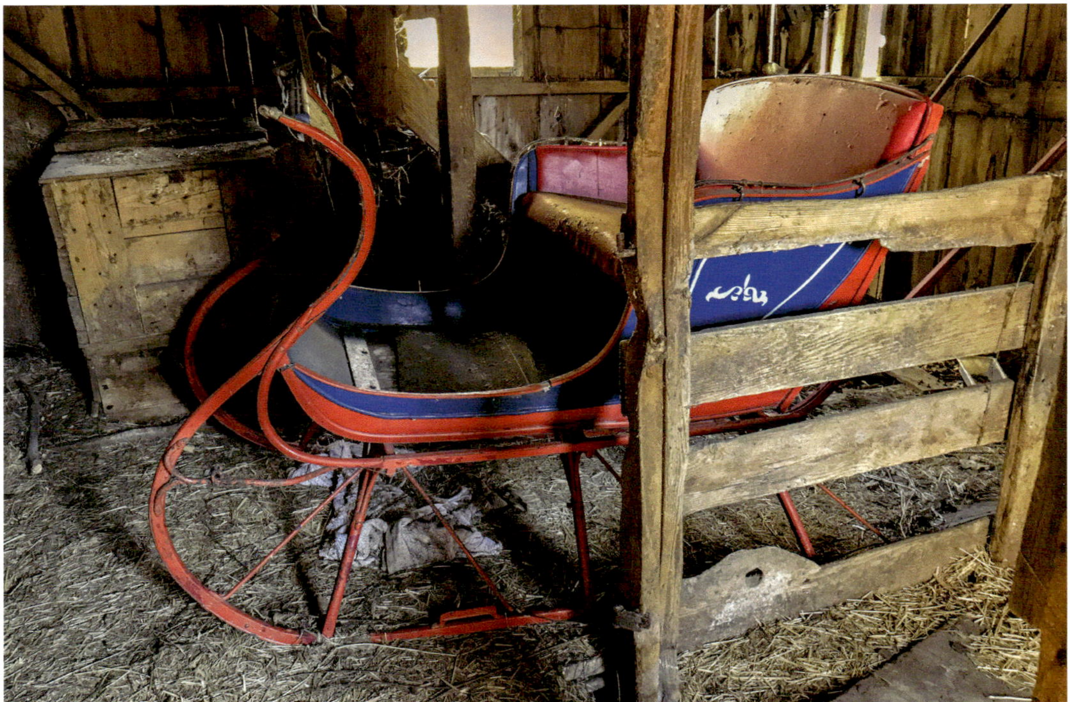

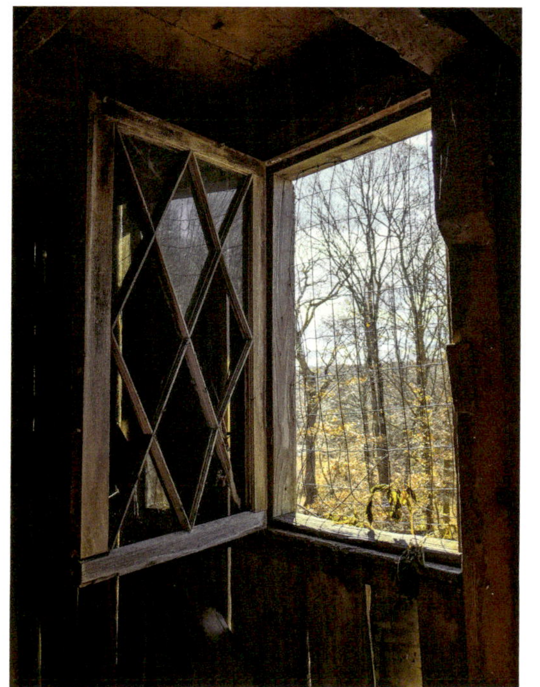

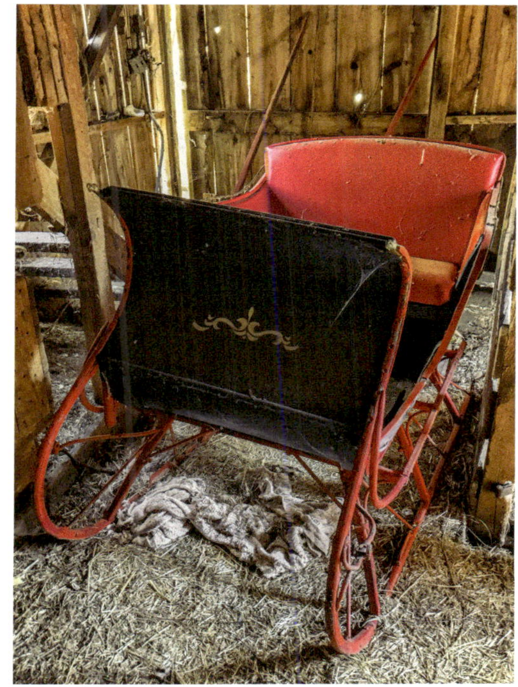

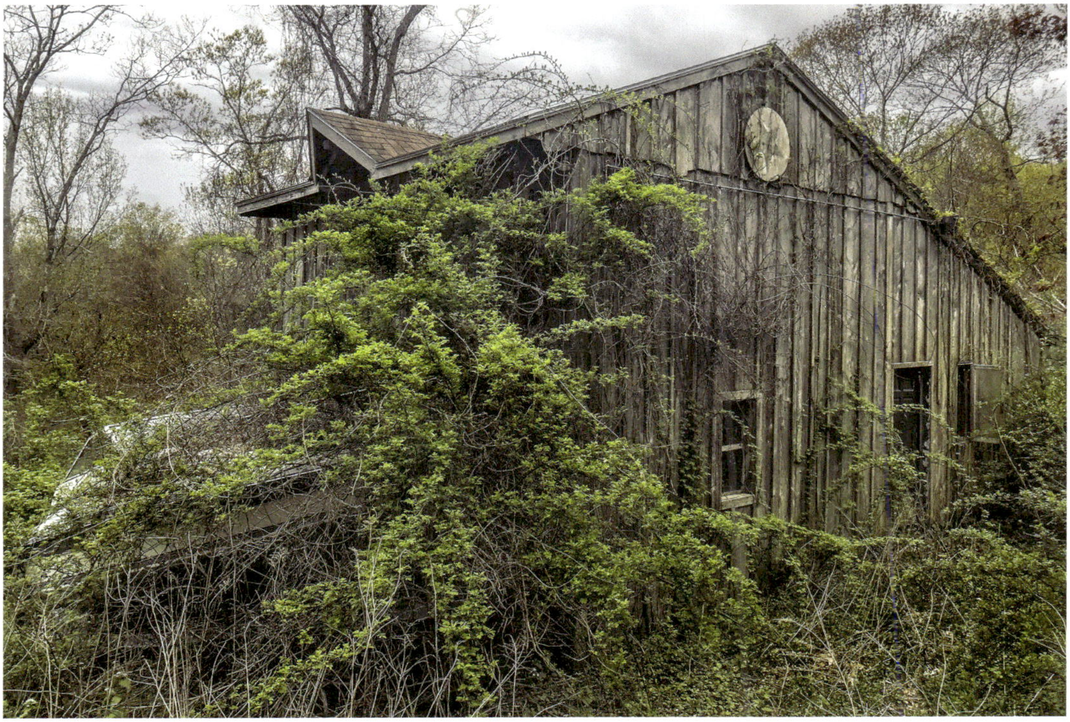

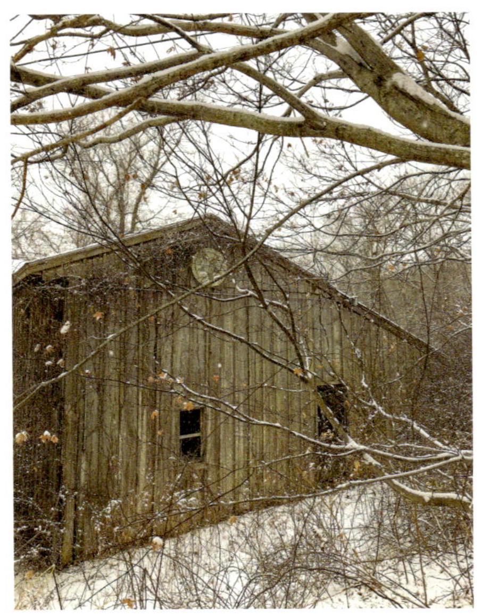 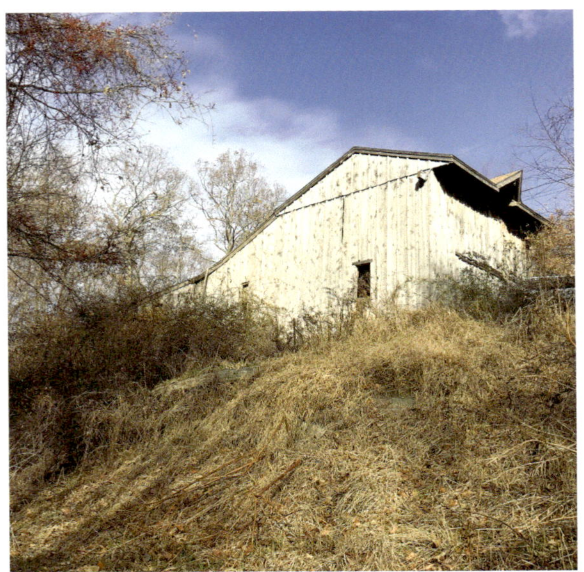

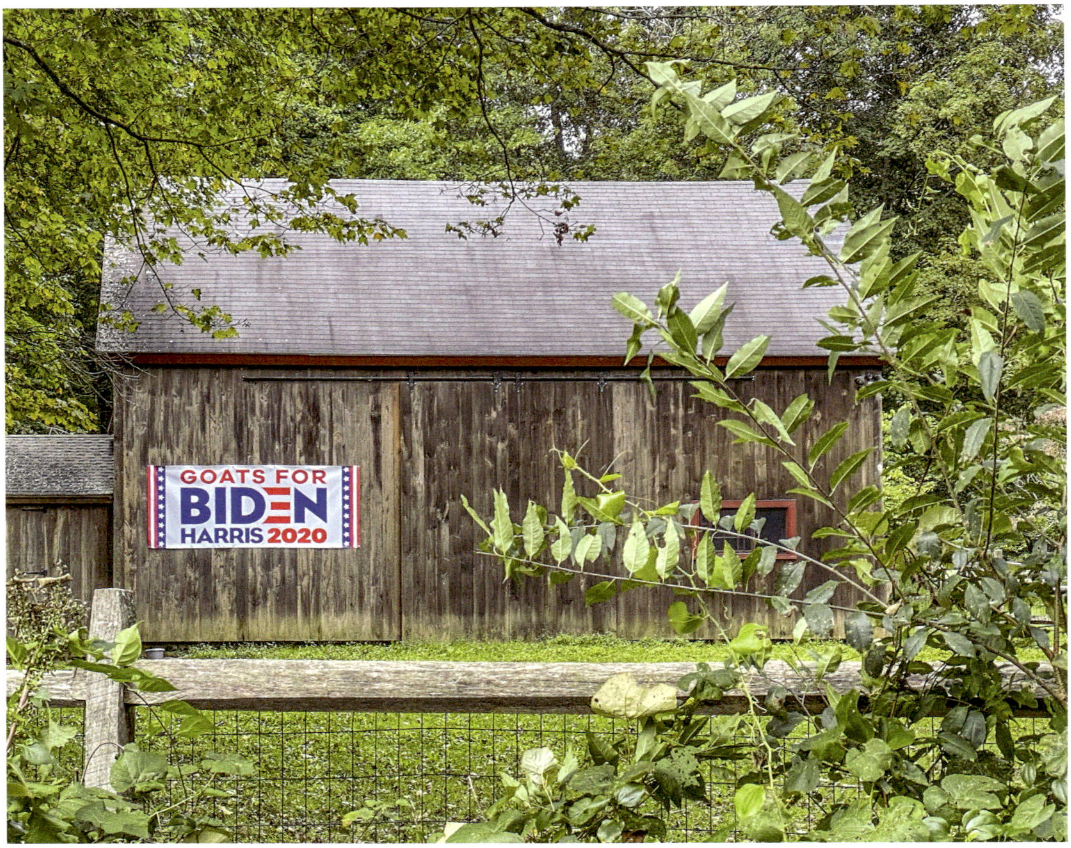

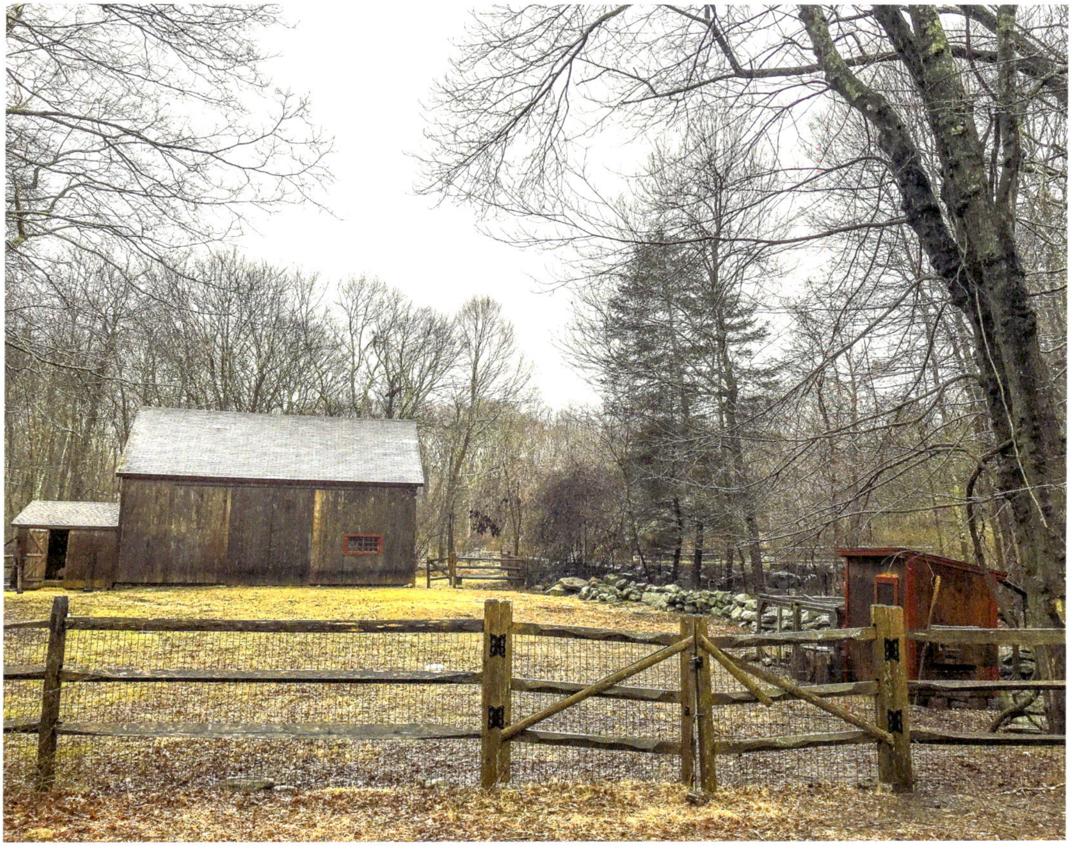

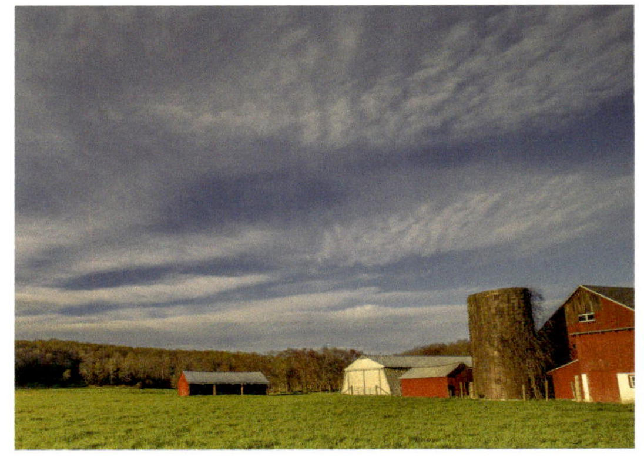

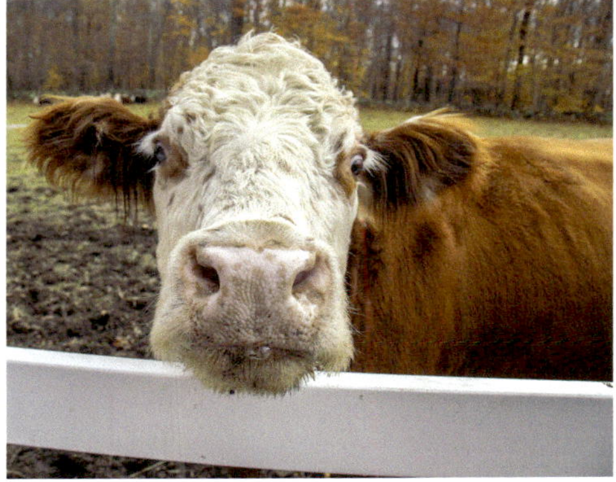

Parmalee Farm

Parmalee Farm offers public open space, hiking trails, community gardens, and a maple sugar house. Patrons can participate in numerous activities offered throughout the season. Car shows with local music, learning how to make maple syrup, Halloween pumpkin carving, community yard and bake sales, Owl-O-Ween put on by local raptor rescue, A Place Called Hope, weddings, and parties are just some of the fun that happens there.

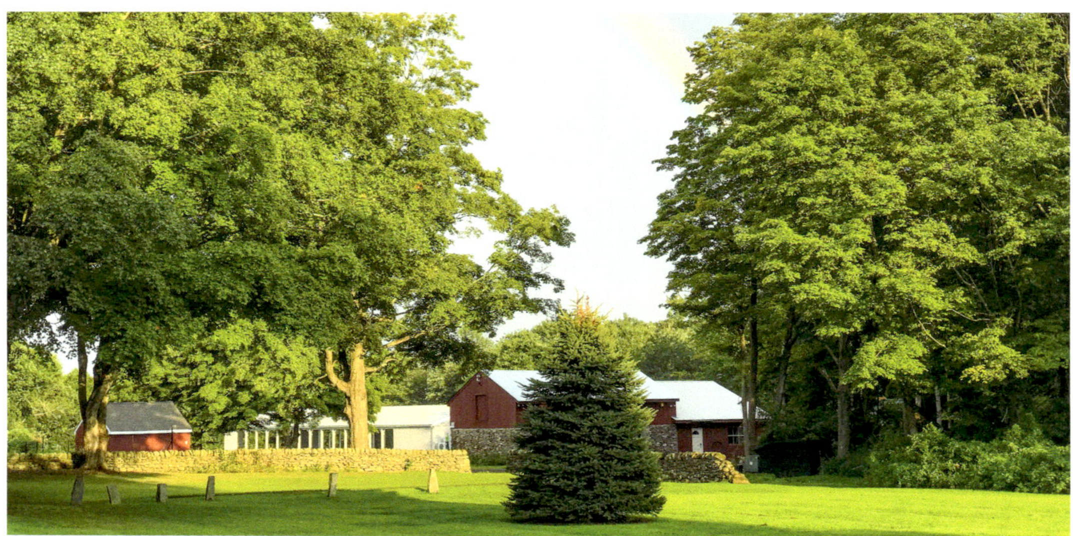

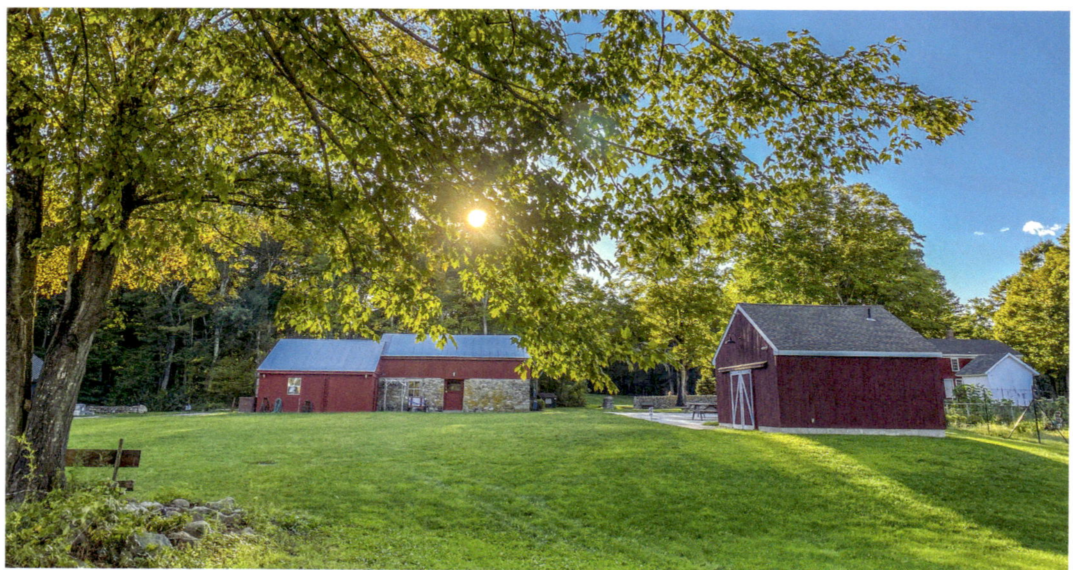

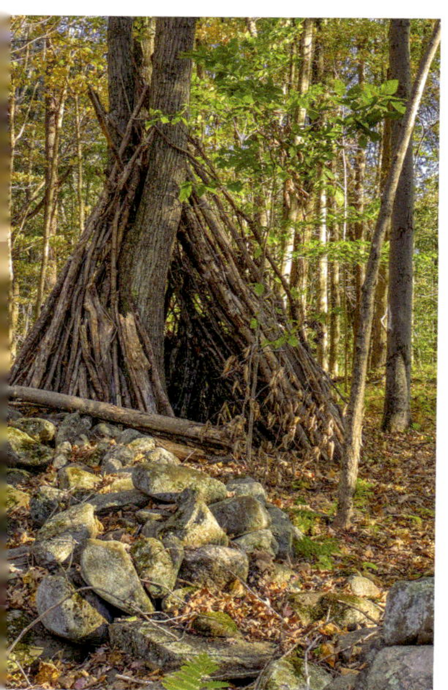 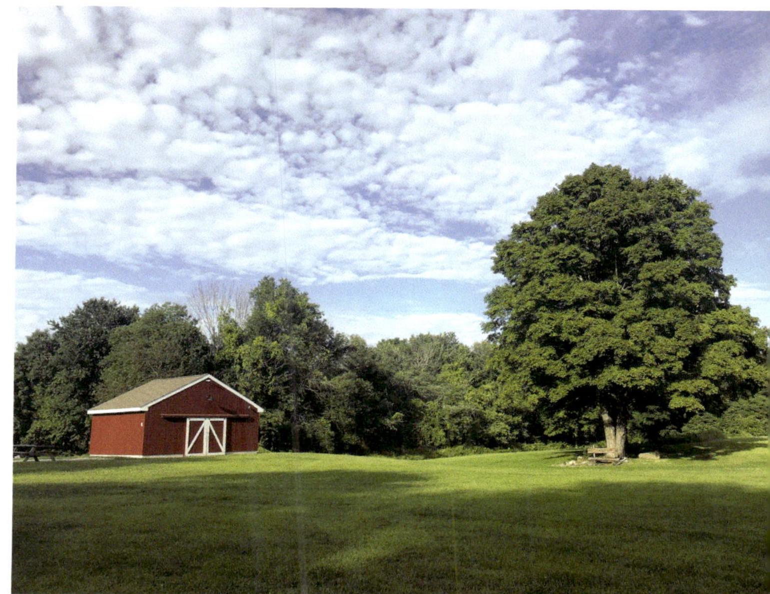

Running Brook Farm

Running Brook Farm is an excellent example of a farm moving into the future. This establishment sells a variety of native plants, flowers, and vegetables, along with many exotics. The interior now houses a charming coffee and tea shop. Local goods, raw wood slabs, and art are featured throughout. The staple crop is hemp, and Running Brook offers many CBD and hemp products. Fresh Christmas trees and numerous seasonal and holiday collections decorate the property.

Overlook Farm Stand

Farm stands have made a resurgence as of late. Found on large farms featuring vegetables or residences selling their hydrangea blooms, they are all different, colorful, and show immense personality. Recently, Overlook Farm went on the market, listing its 1789 antique Cape Cod home and 12.9 acres for a whopping $1,050,000. The listing states there are Long Island Sound views from the front porch. Farm homes have come a long way.

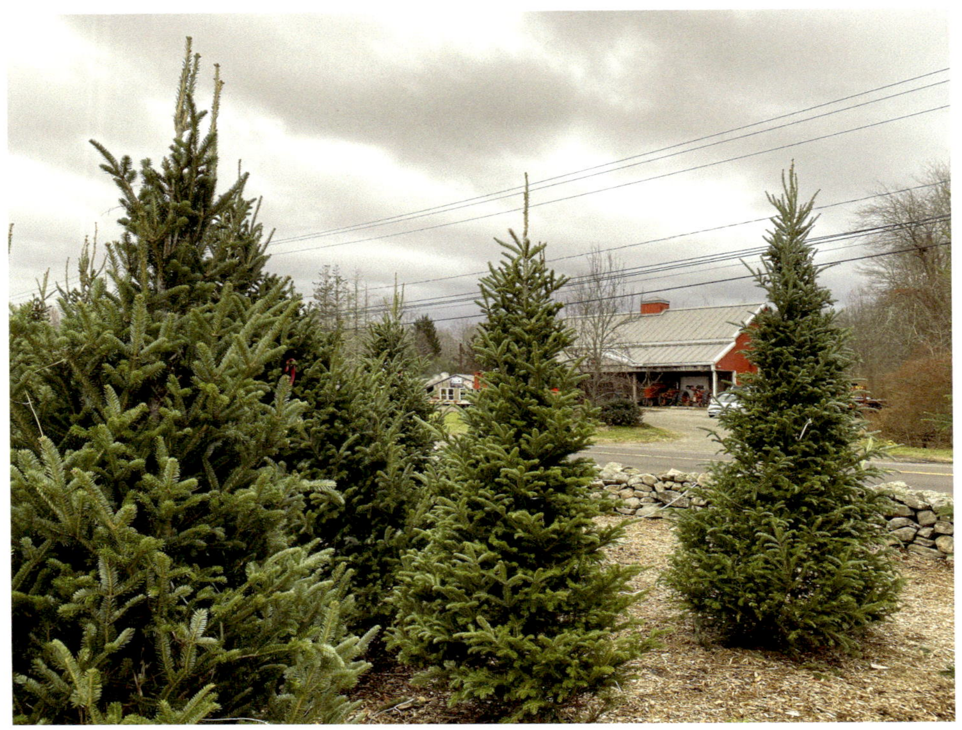

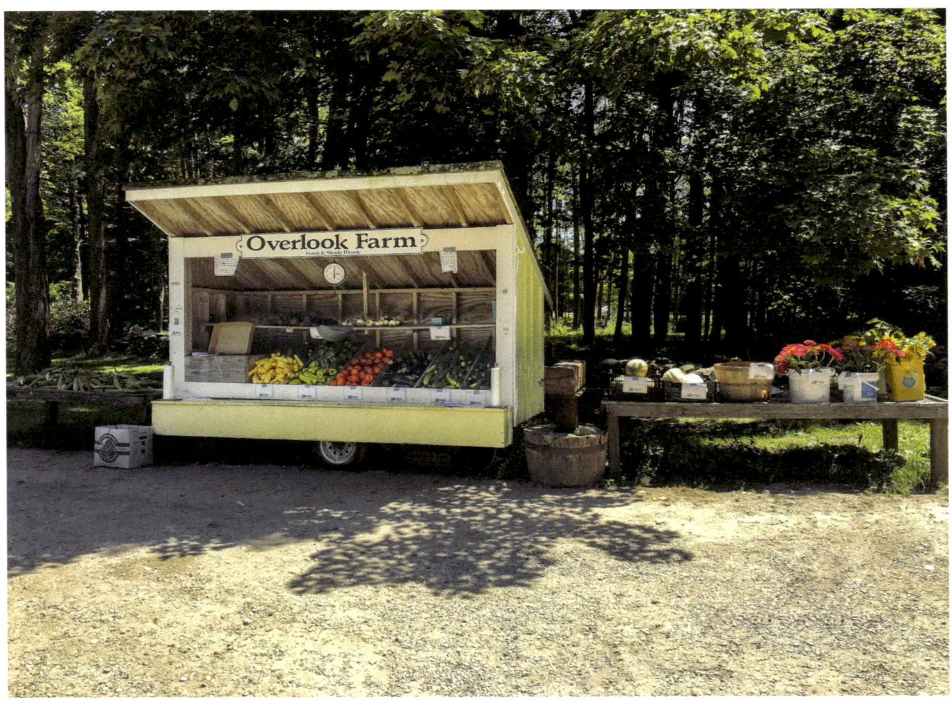

Overlook Farm

Leightsinger Farm and Farm Stand

Leightsinger Farm and Farm Stand is a Killingworth staple run by a friendly townie family, the Rickerts, and named for Mary Rickert's grandmother. Yearly, they participate in the town's farm day, giving everyone a look at their livestock and meat tastings, along with meeting some of the fun, treat-motivated animals. Until recently, Leightsinger Farm ensured the residents had fresh vegetables and eggs daily with their farm stand along Route 81—the farmstand started by Mary and her daughter, Jessica. Jessica succumbed to cancer, but Mary pushed on with the stand in her memory until somebody robbed them four consecutive times. Despite a town behind them and numerous donations, they still chose, in 2021, to close the Leightsinger's stand. These are things that consumers don't consider when a business uses the honor system and a secured cash box. It is not just $250 here and there but the farmer's livelihood. Farming is hard work, and you must sell a lot of cucumbers to make those numbers. Incidents like this can be devastating, mainly if it occurs multiple times. If anything, it is more discouraging to want to continue.

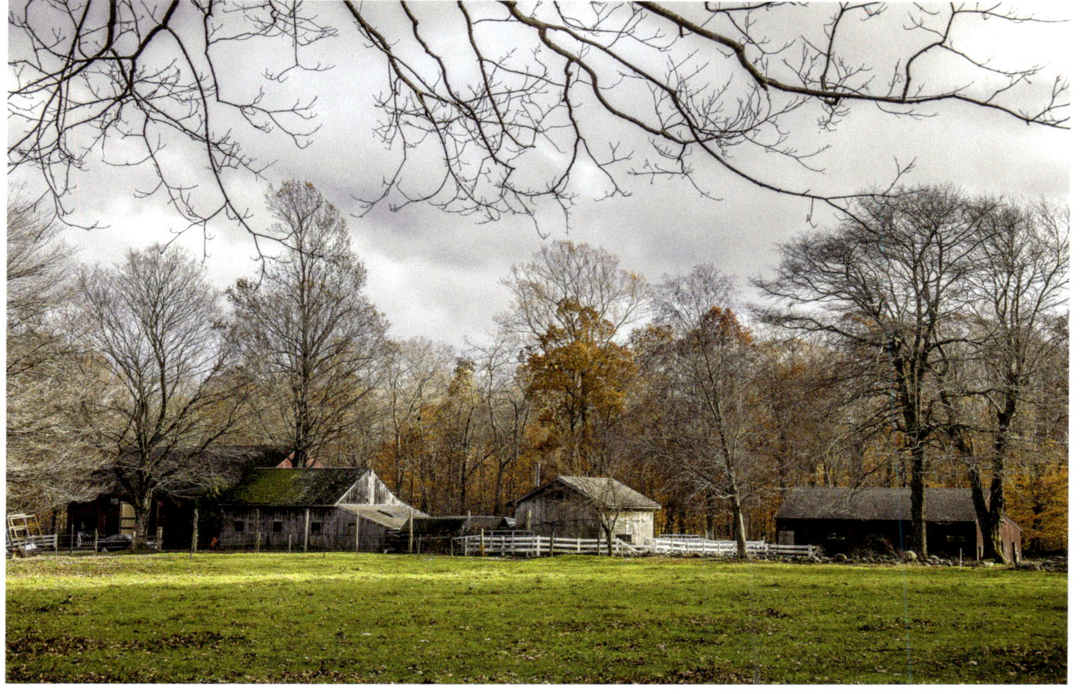

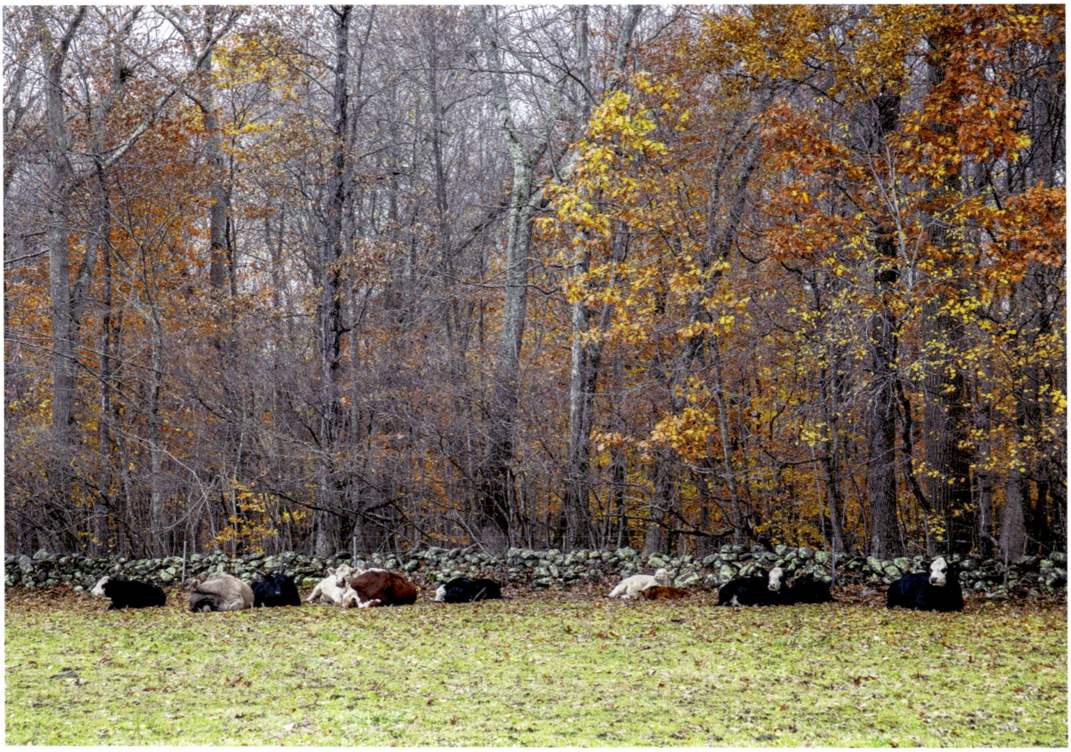

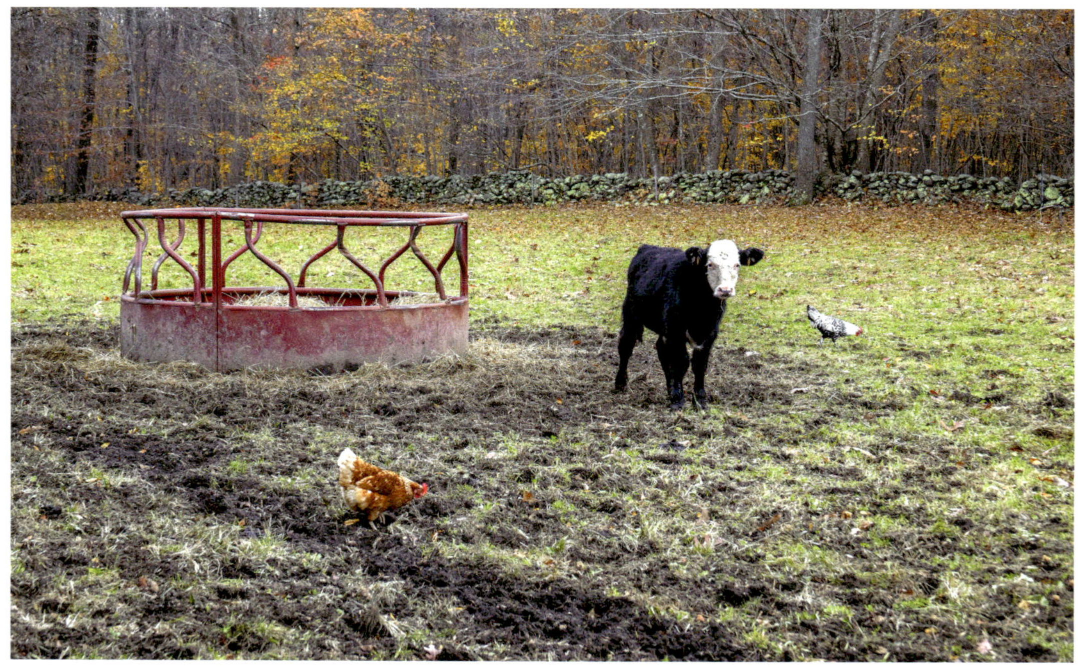

Sweet William Farm

Sweet William Farm is named for the mule with pizzaz and a big personality. Sweet William rules the roost, and his antics are a joy to discover. Pigs, Fang and Franklin; cows, Chloe and Copper; goats, sheep, chickens, and a wily escape artist calf reside on this hobby farm at 400 Roast Meat Hill Road in Killingworth. In addition to selling wool and eggs, Kim Marie and Robert rescue dogs, pot belly pigs, geese, and ducks.

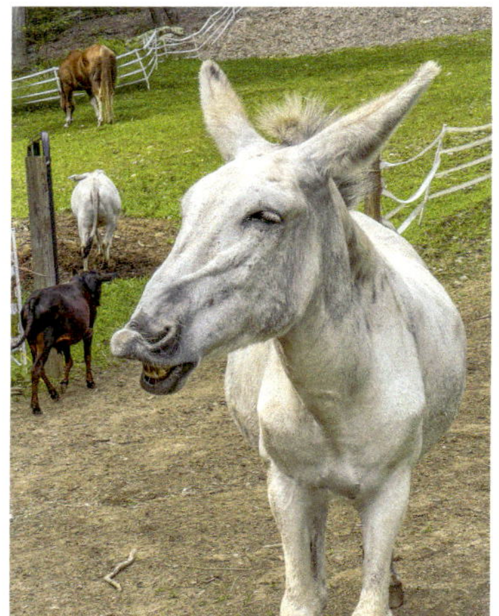
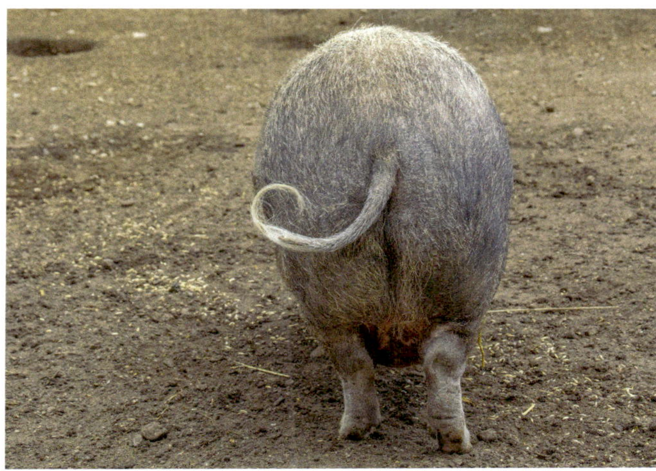

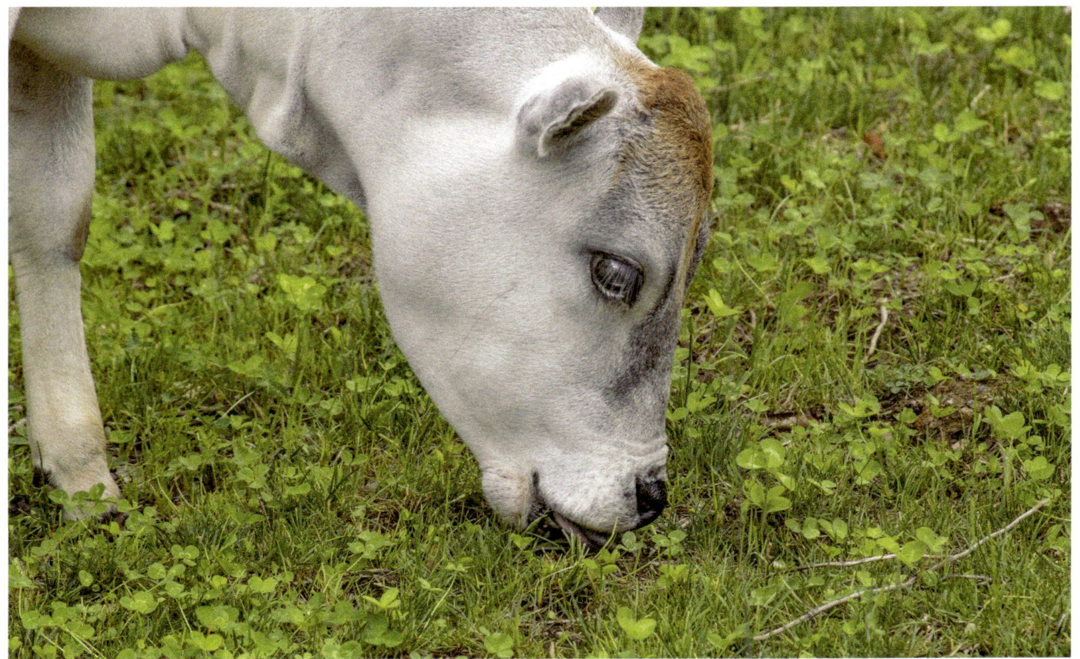

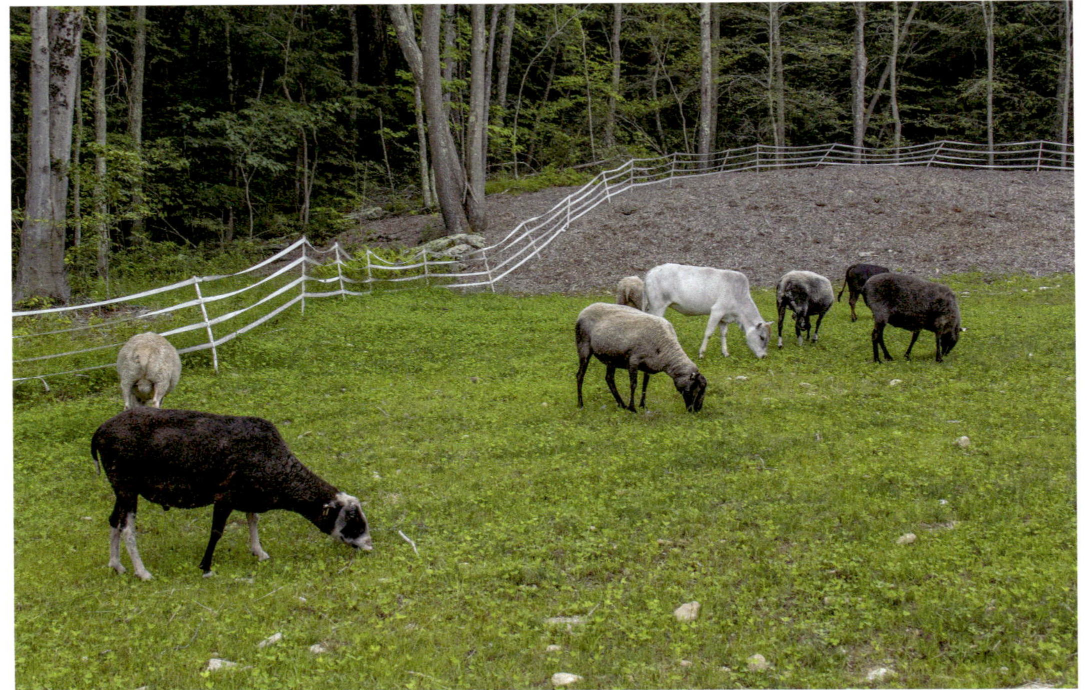

Alpacas

Alpacas are abundant for farming nationwide, and Killingworth is no different. It is estimated there are about 53,000 Alpaca farms in the United States. 2,915 of these Alpacas reside in Connecticut and consist of Suri and Huacaya breeds. Two of Connecticut's Alpaca farms are in Killingworth.

New England Alpacas, located at 14 Bethke Road in Killingworth, has an Alpaca Farm and an Alpaca Farm Store on the property. The store offers a high-end variety of mittens, gloves, hats, scarves, sweaters, socks, boot inserts, toys, nature-inspired items, fiber, yarns, and roving. They broke out the technology during farm days and showed us how to spin the wool. In recent years, they have also had felting demonstrations. As you can guess, Alpacas have silly personalities and can be temperamental at times but almost always offer a giggle no matter what.

Tucked in the pine and deciduous trees of Killingworth bordering Madison, Connecticut, Para Siempre Alpacas has given me more joy than I can describe. Nothing is funnier than when the Alpacas come out for breakfast. They have rolled down hills, taken dust baths, chased each other, munched pine trees with twisted lips, and generally been silly, for lack of a better word. Silly faces, silly antics, and foolishness, 100% ridiculous, are the best ways to describe these beasts. Only a few things are available in the information about Para Siempre Alpacas. Other than that, they are eco-friendly, environmentally sound, socially conscious, and entertaining as all get out!

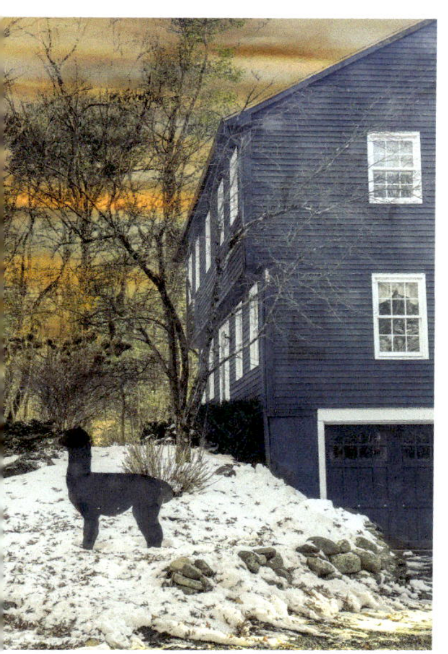

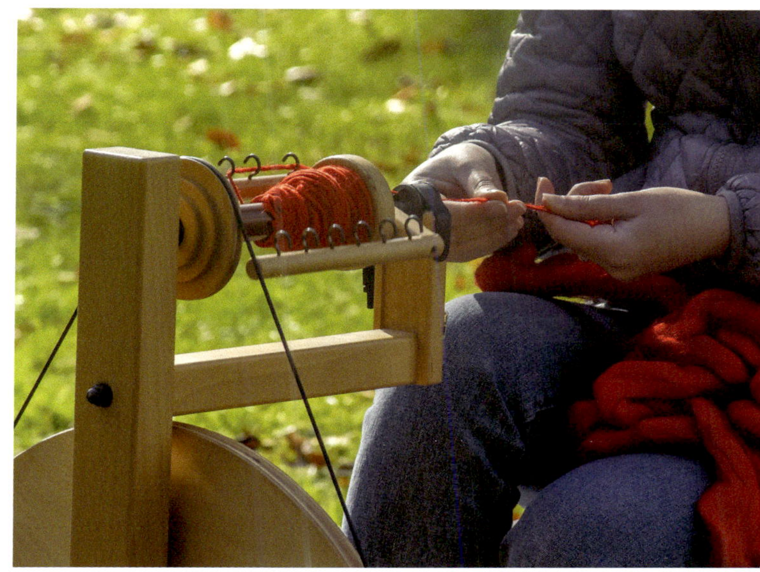

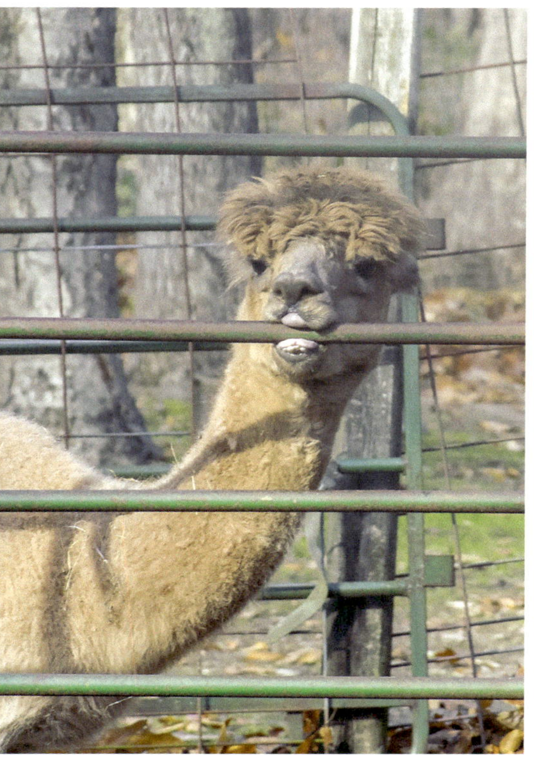

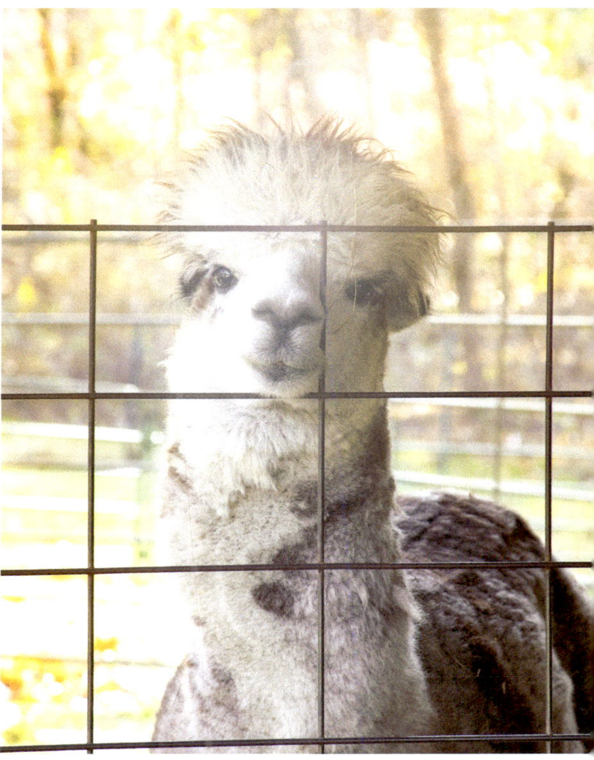

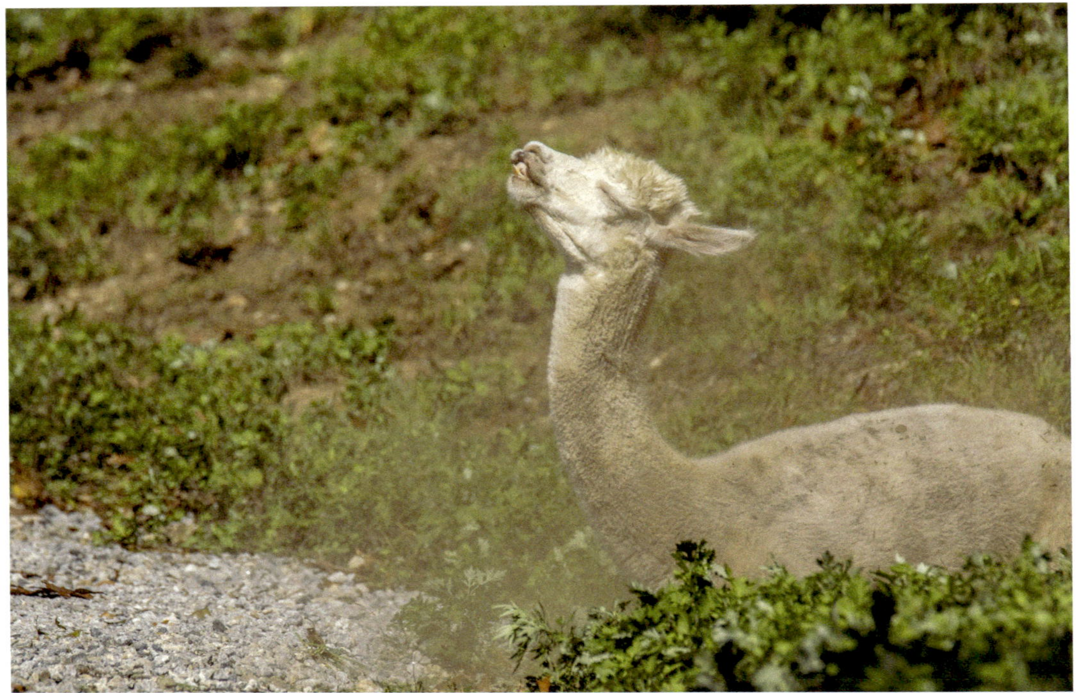

Bauer Farm, Madison

I have spent more than 100 days here on Bauer Farm. It is one place that made my life in Connecticut very special. Throughout the year, any number of native and vagrant birds appear. The community gardens are one of the most stunning I have ever visited. Butterflies and insects dance on the variety of petals raised in each plot. Trails around grasslands surround the acreage. One could see a dog show at any given time as there is always a variety of pups to be found on leash. Wetlands, Ponds, and a covered bridge decorate the low country. Seasonal activities and a harvest day for the surrounding areas are consistent. There is a feeling of peacefulness and fulfillment just sitting on a bench watching bunnies and monarch butterflies flit about.

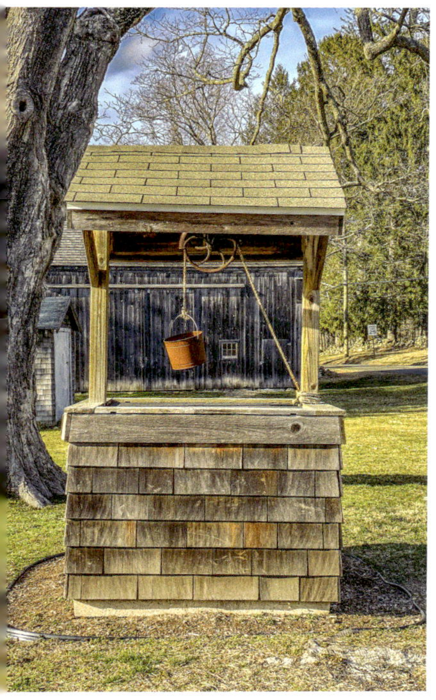

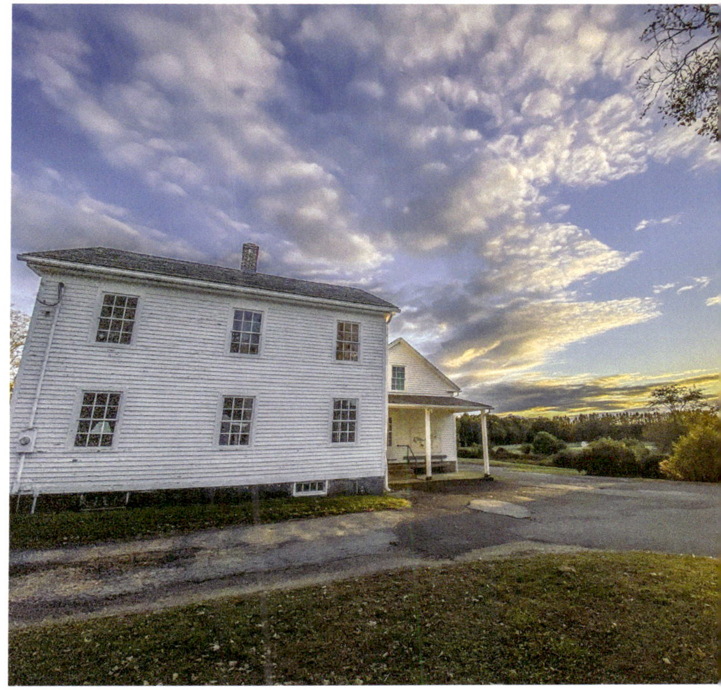

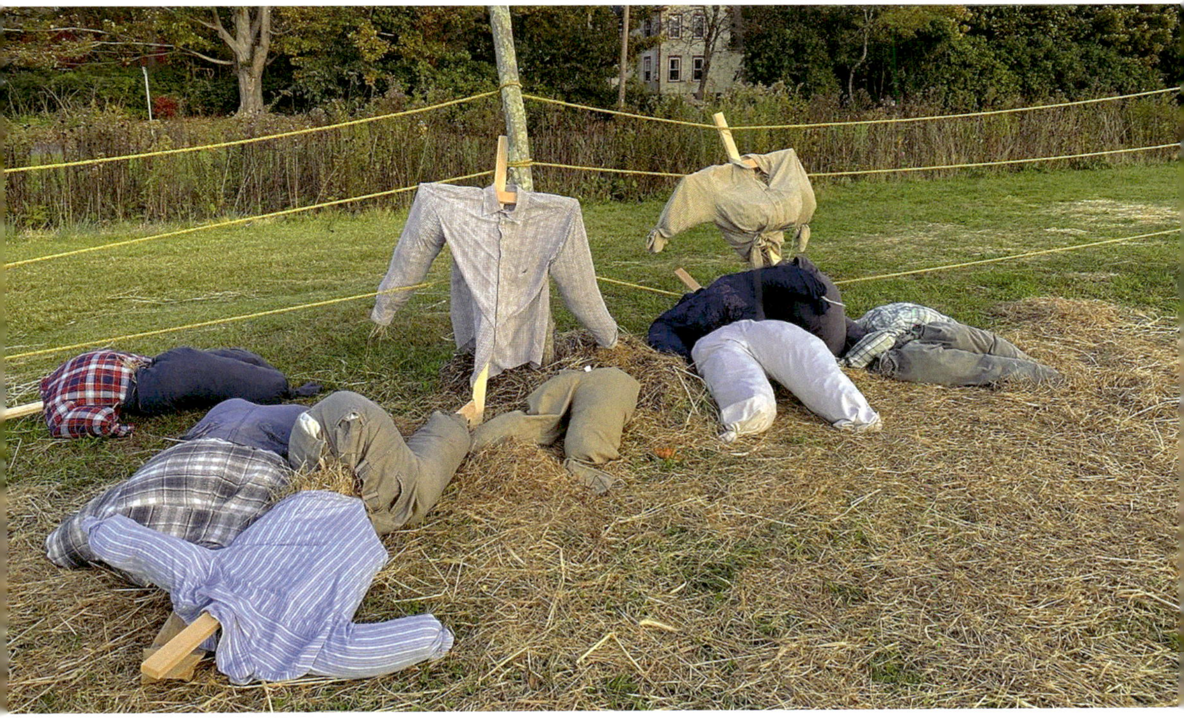

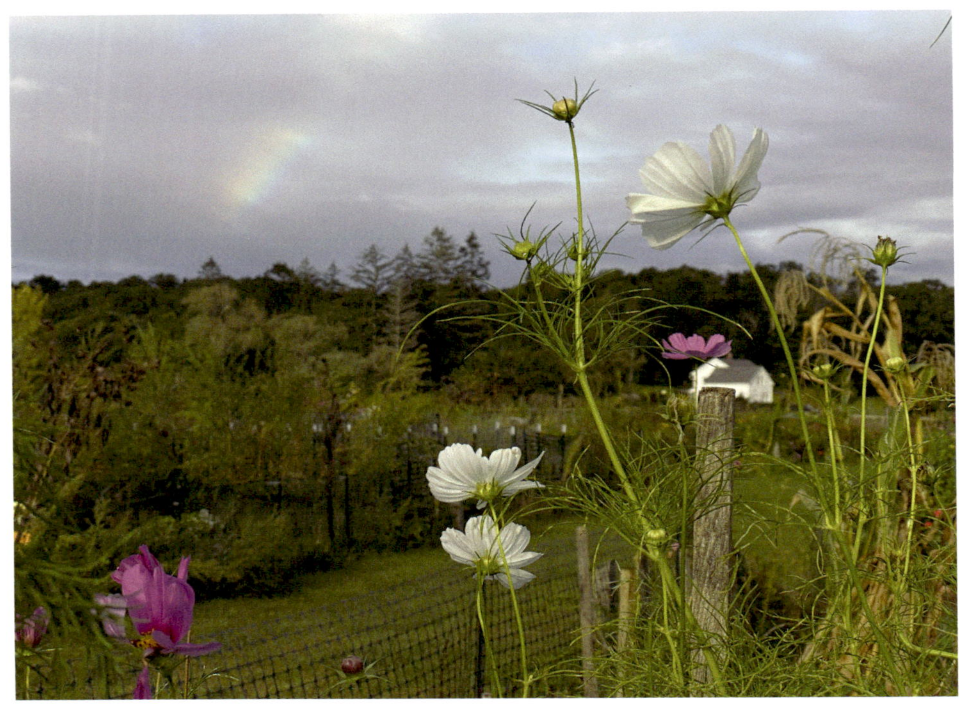

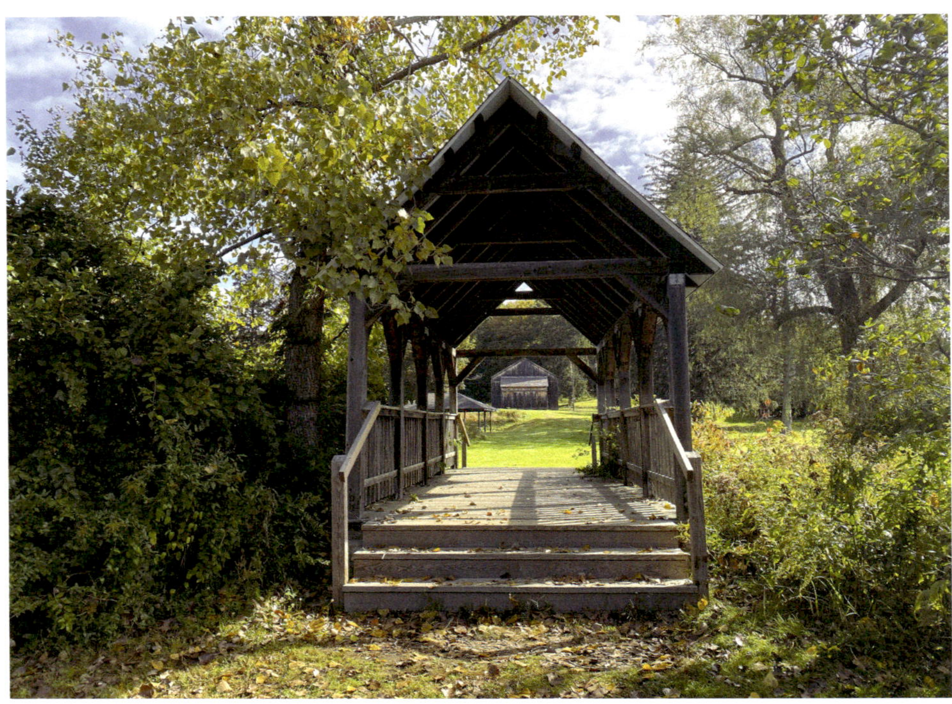

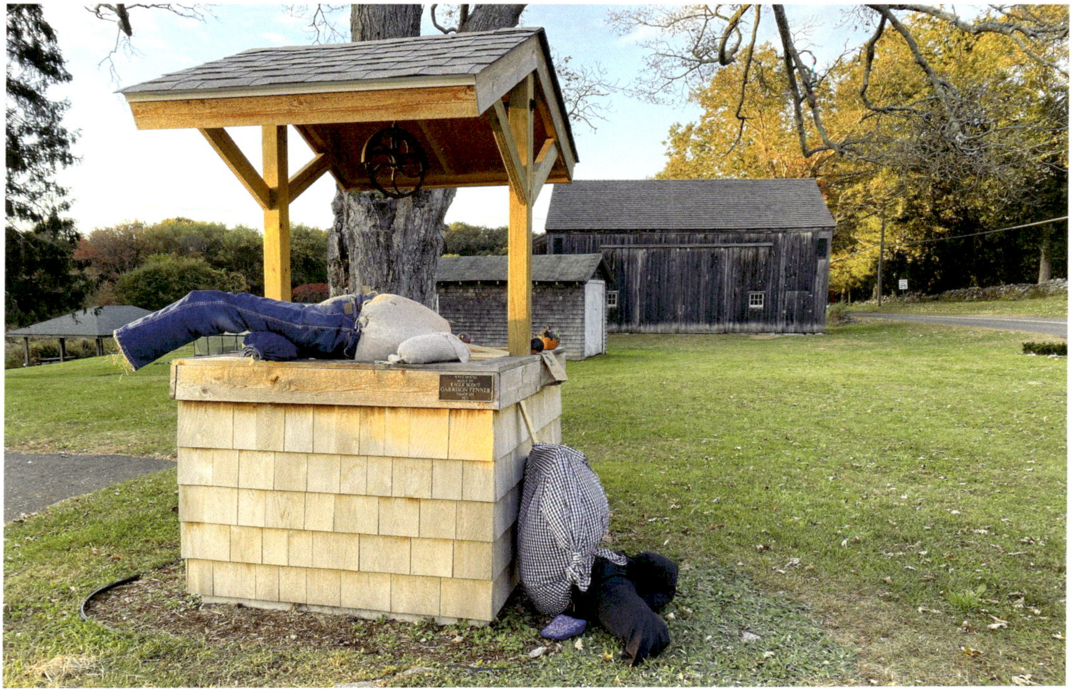
EAGLE SCOUT
GARRISON FENNER

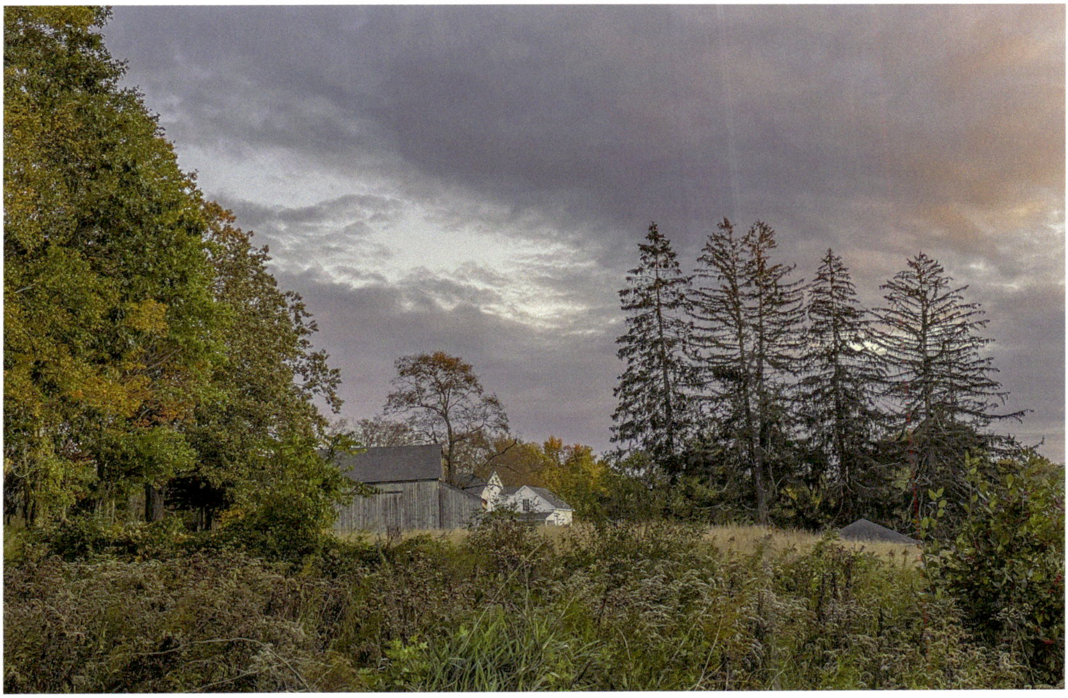

Miscellaneous

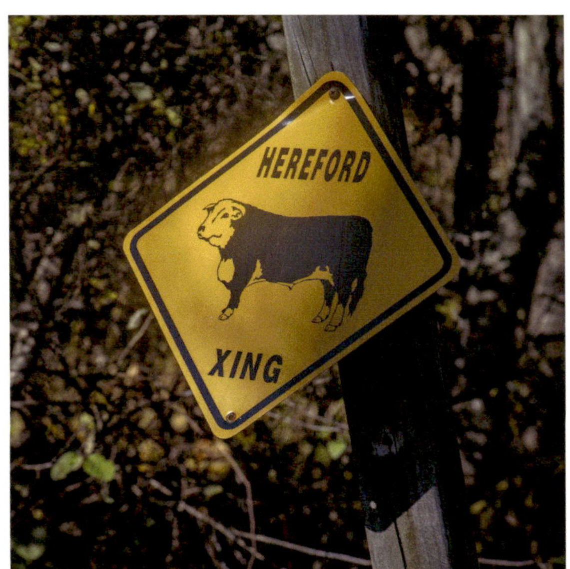

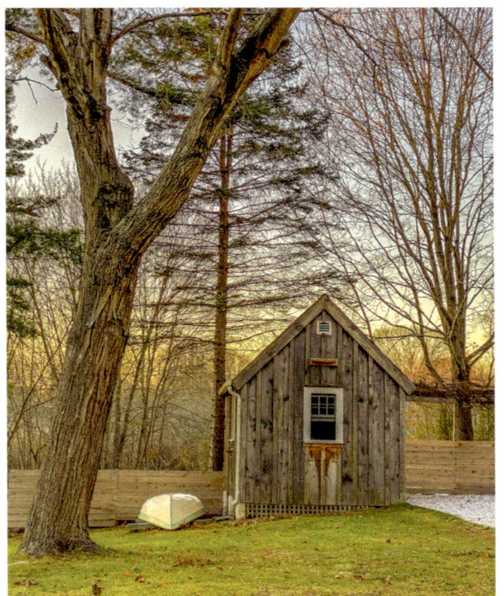

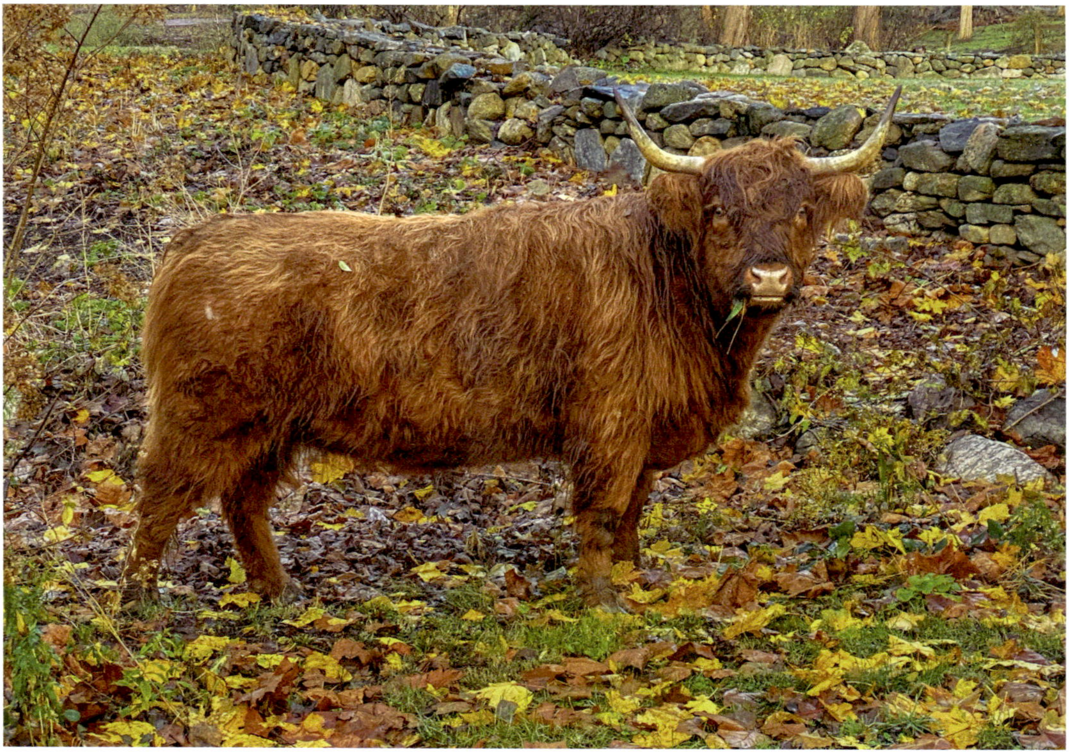

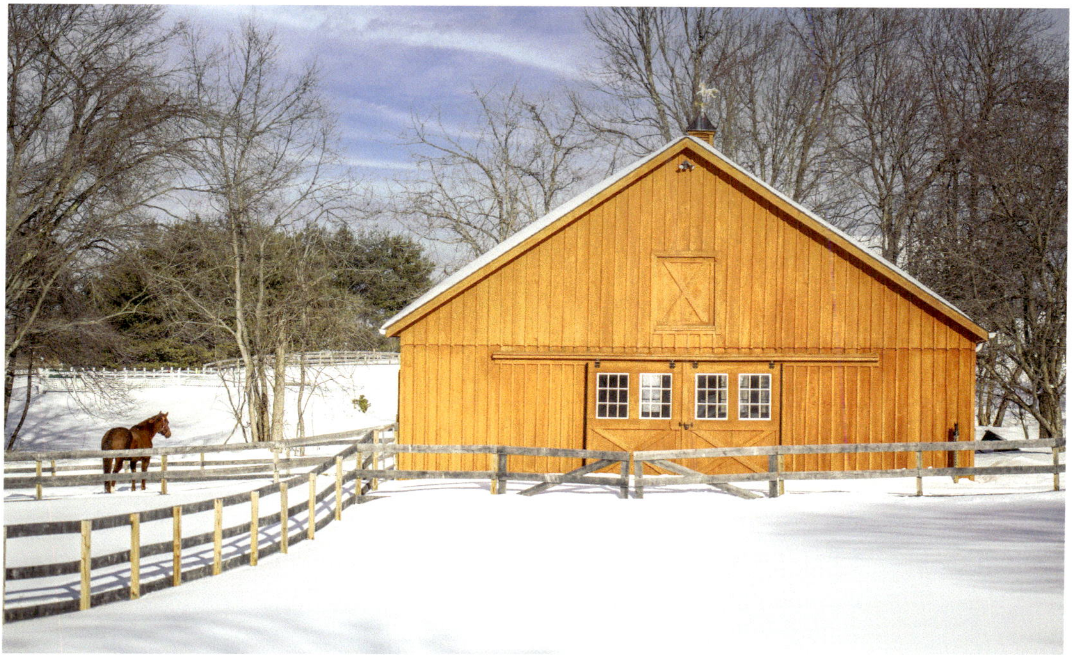

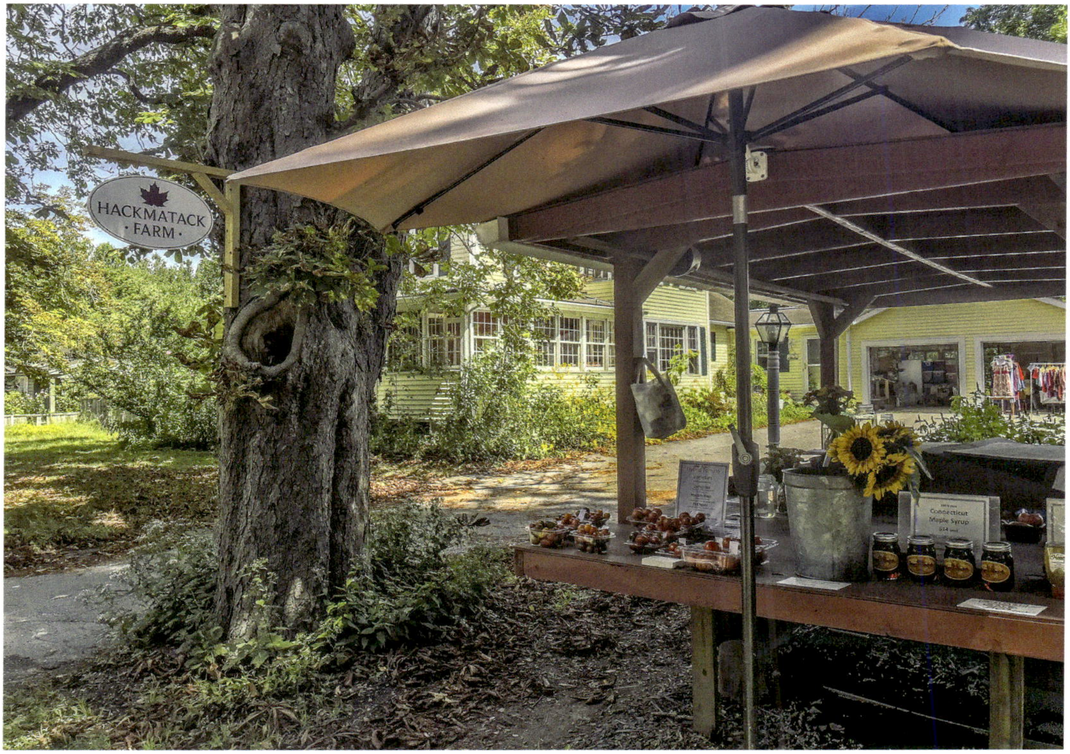
HACKMATACK
· FARM ·
Connecticut
Maple Syrup

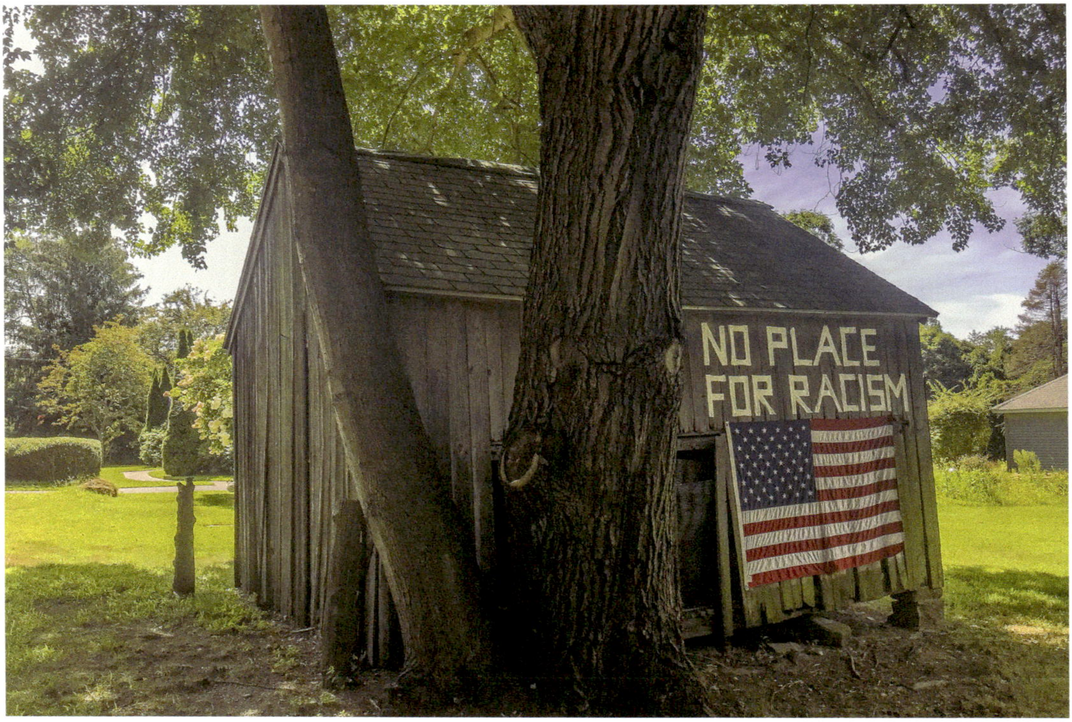

NO PLACE
FOR RACISM

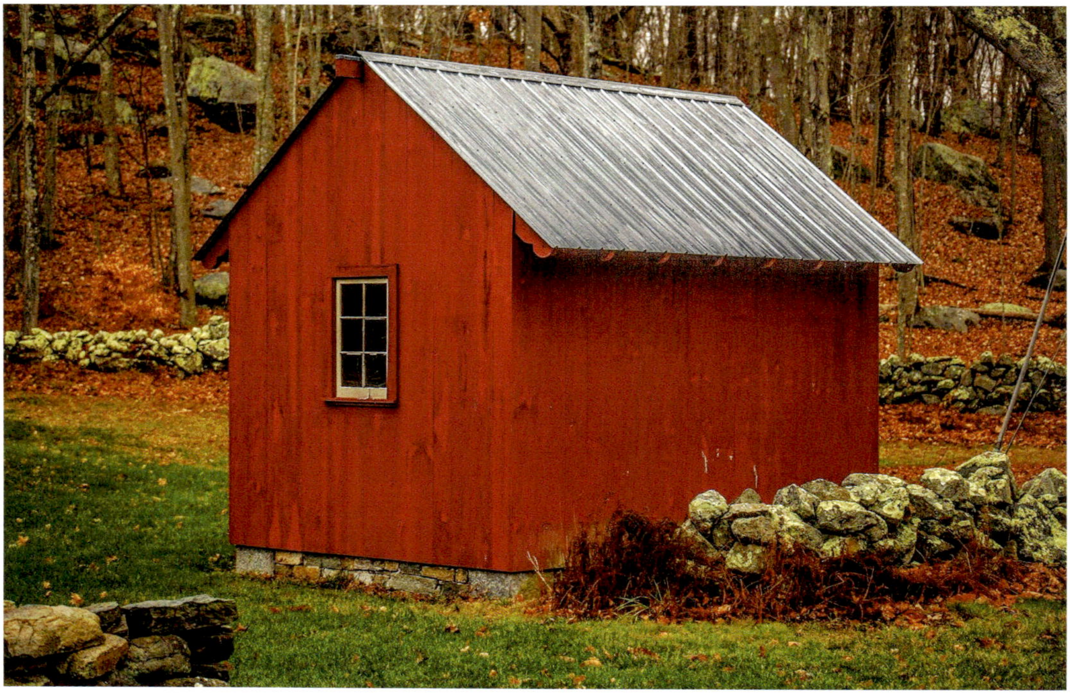

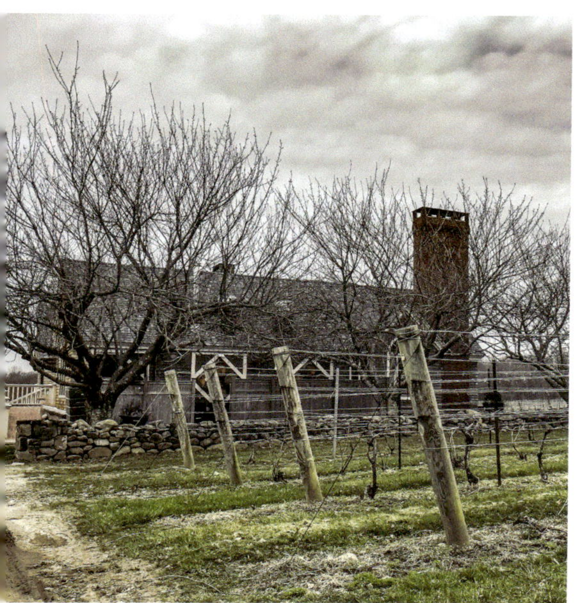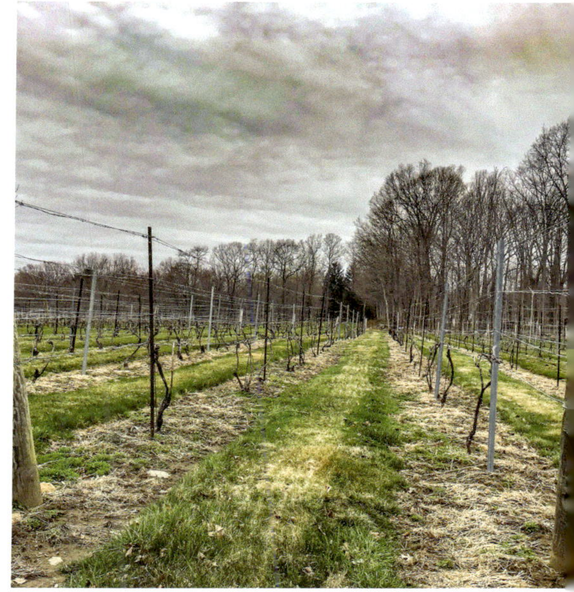

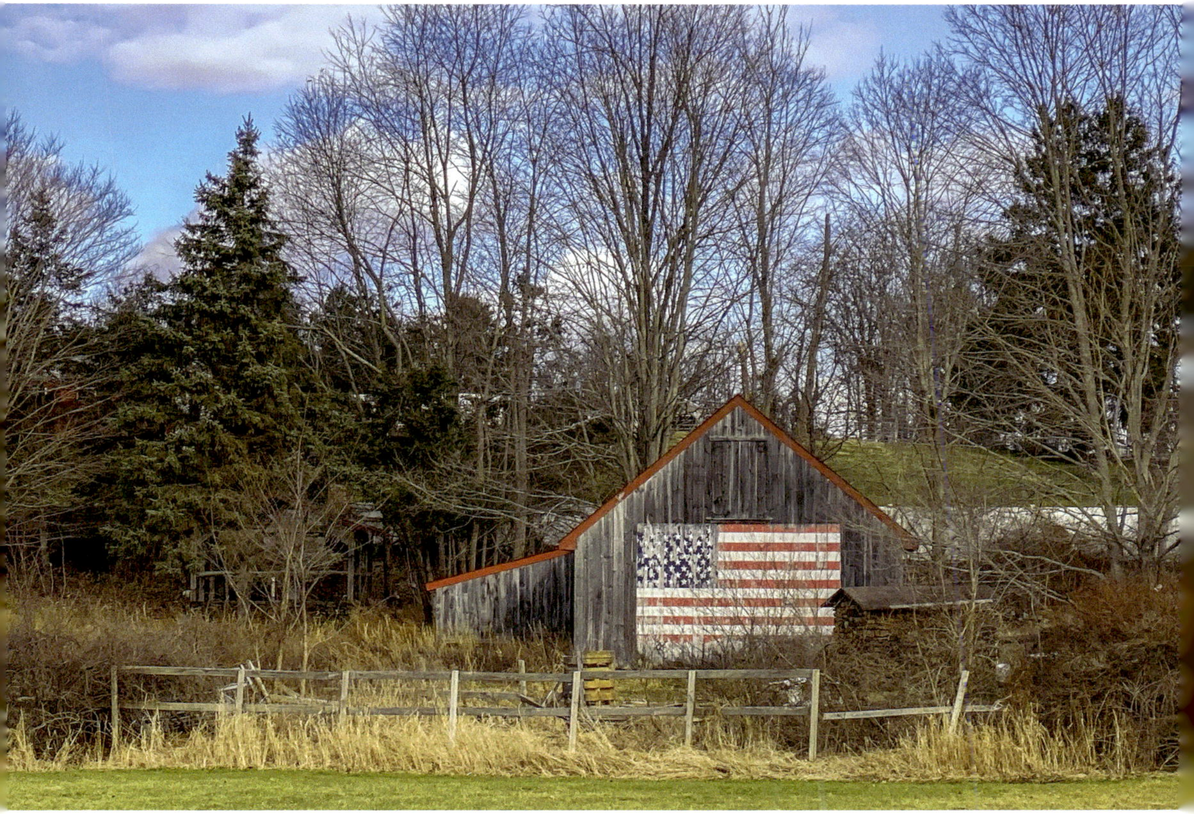

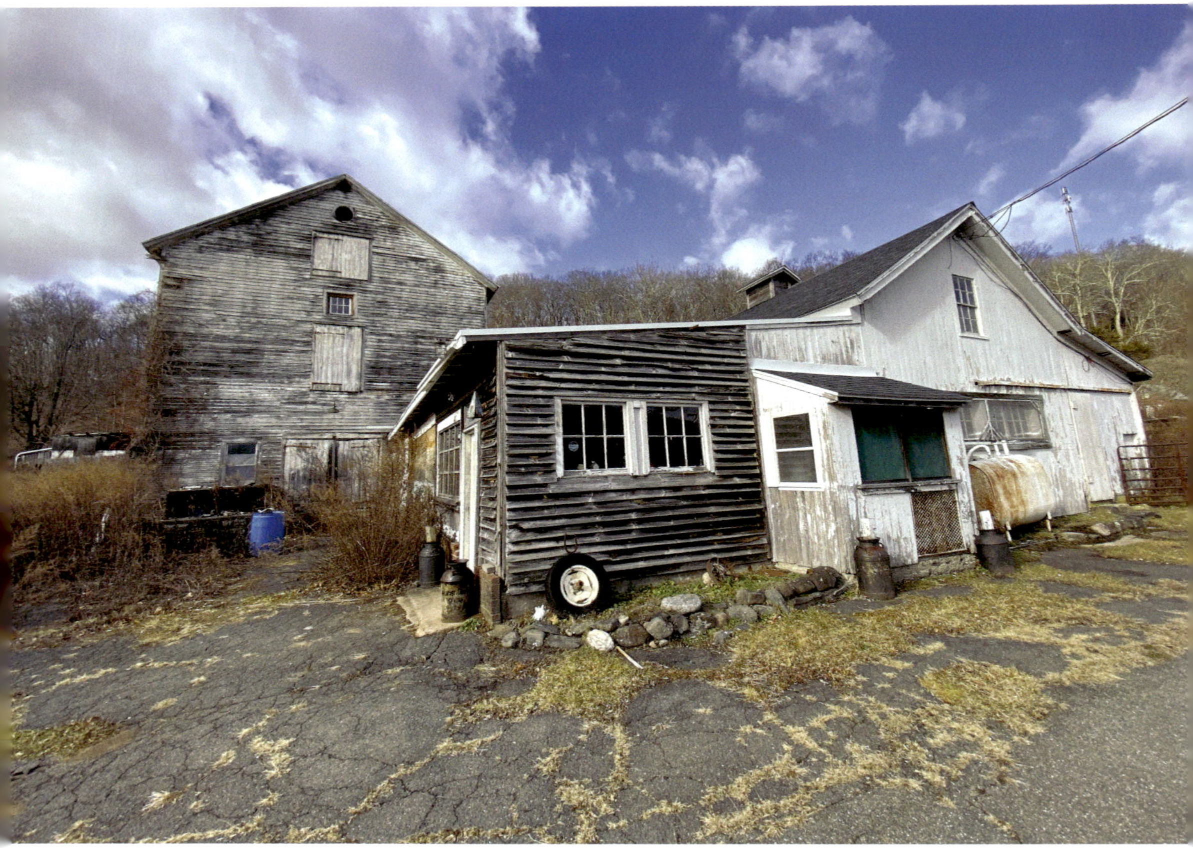

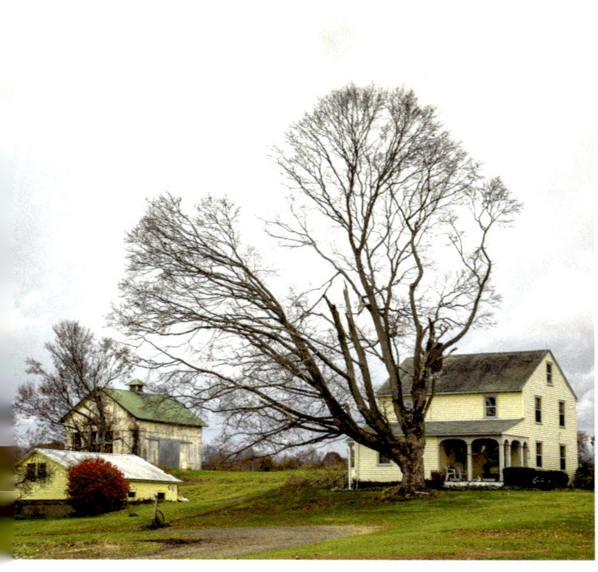

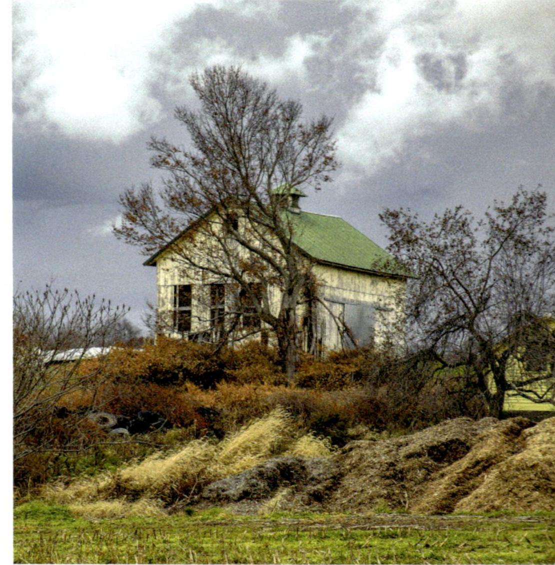

11

Snow's Farm, Easton

Snow's Farm in Easton, CT, has a gambrel-roofed dairy barn surrounded by a working cattle pen offering farm and garden materials from soil and manure to mulch. The same family has operated this farm for 100 years. Today, the farmers are fourth-generation farmers to the 1912 founded freehold.

Shown here are a few of the sweet faces of Fairfield County that reside in Easton. Highland cattle kiss and wiggly piggies play just like puppies. If you have never experienced the personalities of either, I suggest finding a farm that lets you visit and cuddle their creatures. It will change your whole view of both cows and pigs.

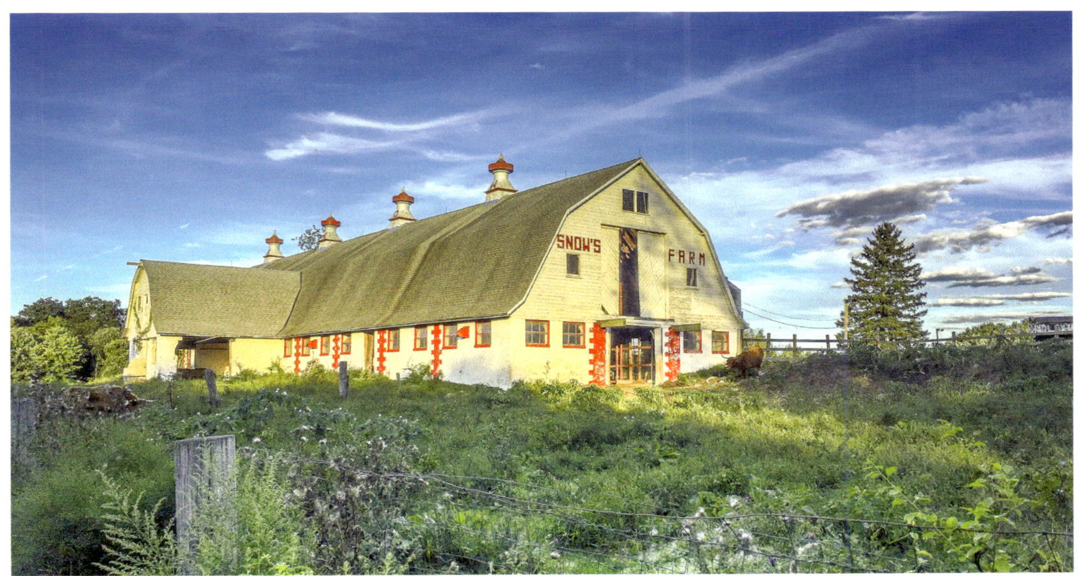

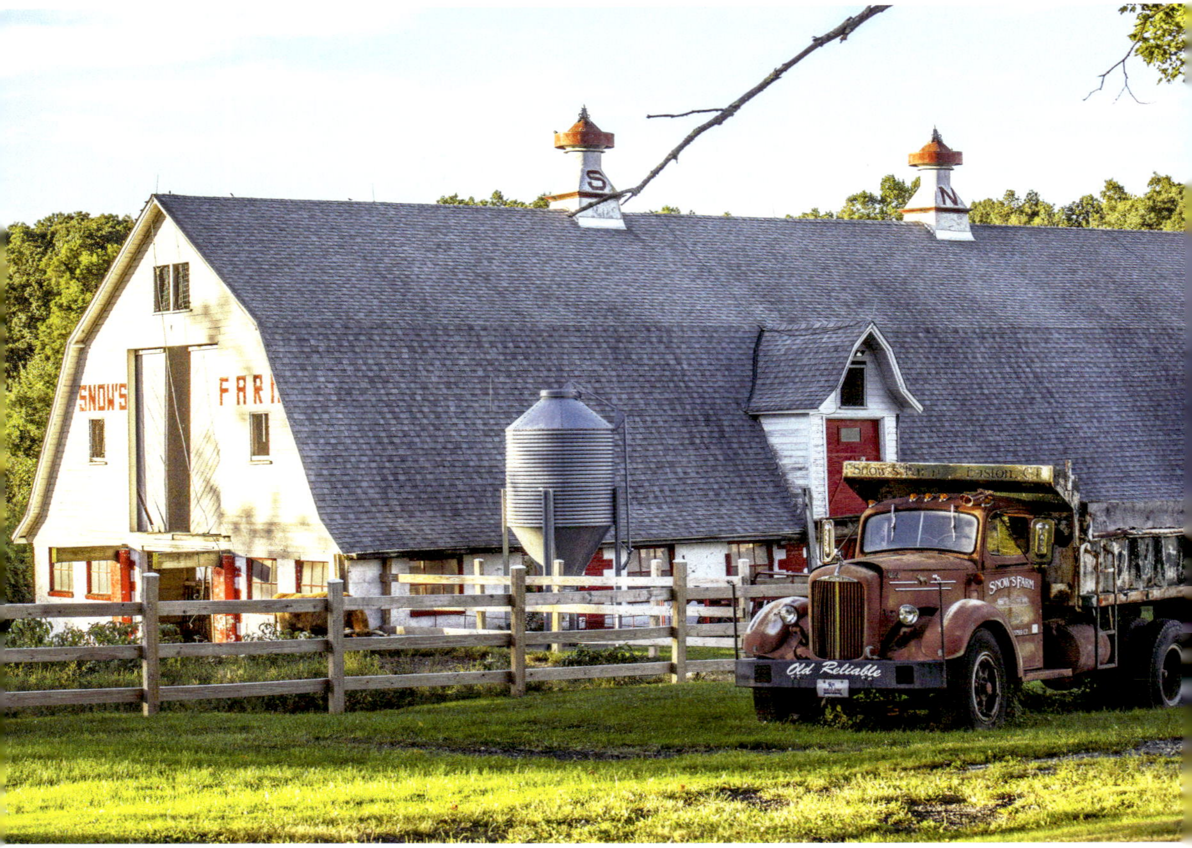

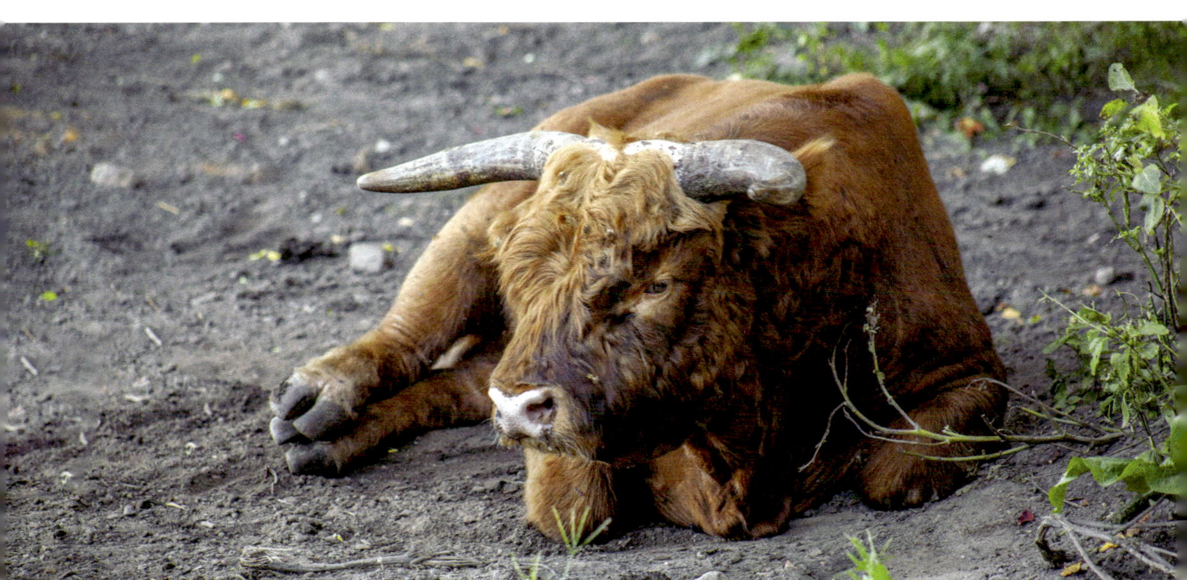
SNOW'S
FARM
Snow's Farm Easton CT
Snow's Farm
Old Reliable

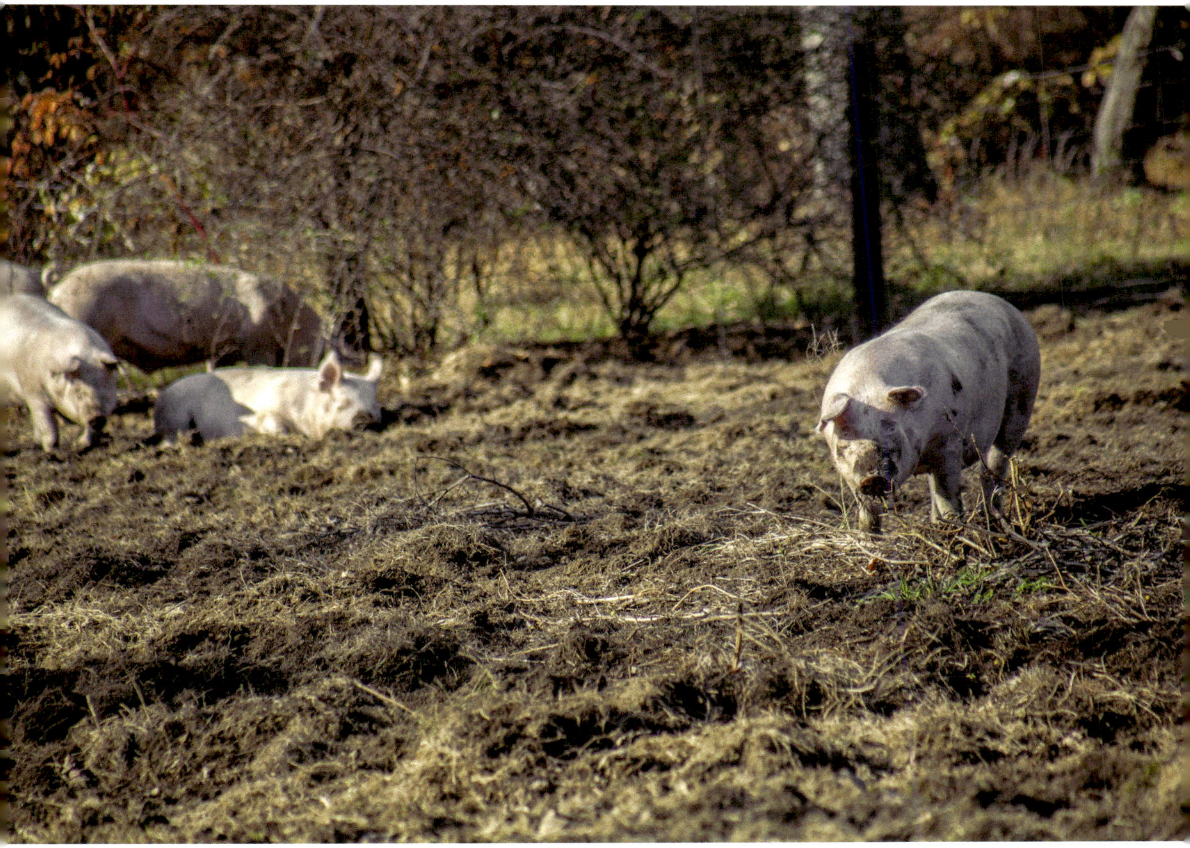

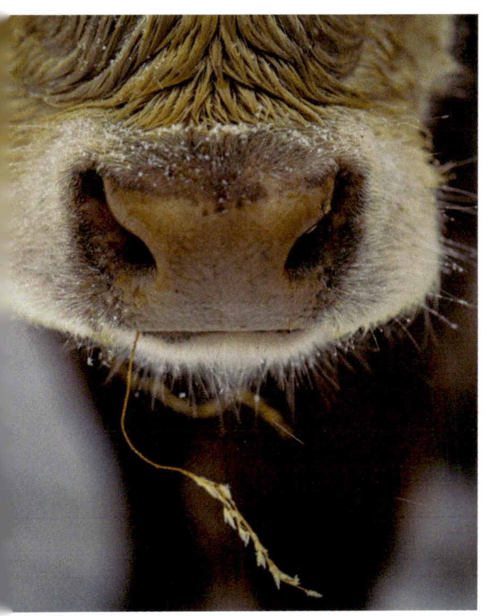

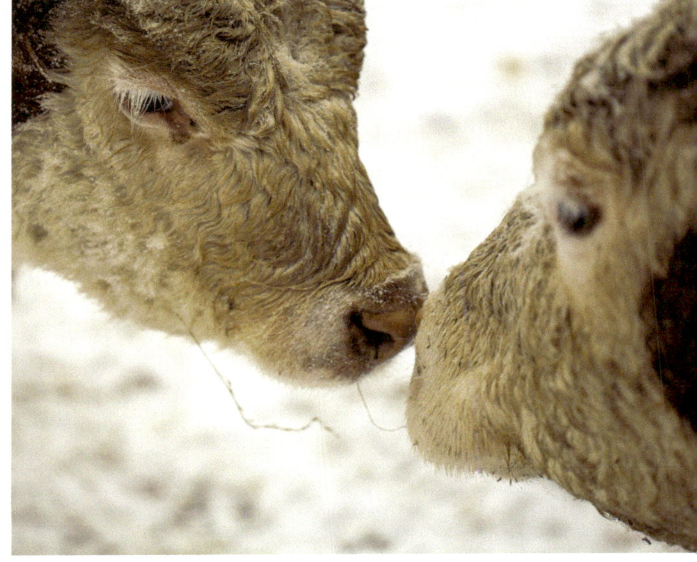

12

Dairy from Cornwall to Litchfield

Bunnell Farm, Litchfield

Bunnell Farm is family-owned and on its fifth generation of farmers. This English bank farm dates back to the 1700s for the older parts of the barn and perhaps the 1800s for the remainder and house. Dairy and horses were the initial uses for this L-shaped barn. Today, the family has made sure they have progressed into modern farming and barn use by offering numerous options for the structure. The barn is available for rent for special occasions such as weddings and parties. A pumpkin patch and corn maze make it a Halloween destination. The corn maze, offered by flashlight at night, is for the ultimate spooks! The labyrinth changes yearly and has ornate patterns that read messages from above, like "We love our Veterans" with a flag or "We love you, Joe!" Hayrides run all day while families select the best pumpkin. Turkeys for Thanksgiving lead to holly and cider for Christmas while offering a variety of homemade holiday gifts for everyone. Bunnells is a one-stop farm experience.

Calf + Clover Creamery, Cornwall

Calf + Clover is another contemporary farm that offers a well-rounded variety of services. The Farm Store is a 365-day, 7 AM to 7 PM honor system venture specializing in raw milk, yogurts, chocolate milk, ricotta, cheese, eggs, beef, and veal. Fruits, veggies, and diverse gifts are available from neighboring farms like Lyric Hill, specializing in goat milk soap. Farm stays with a freshly stocked kitchen and a dairy farm experience are a draw. Calf + Clover has become a picture-perfect, idyllic wedding venue. Previously Stone Wall Dairy, the new owners are committed to continuing on the same path of Stone Wall's strong reputation and historical background.

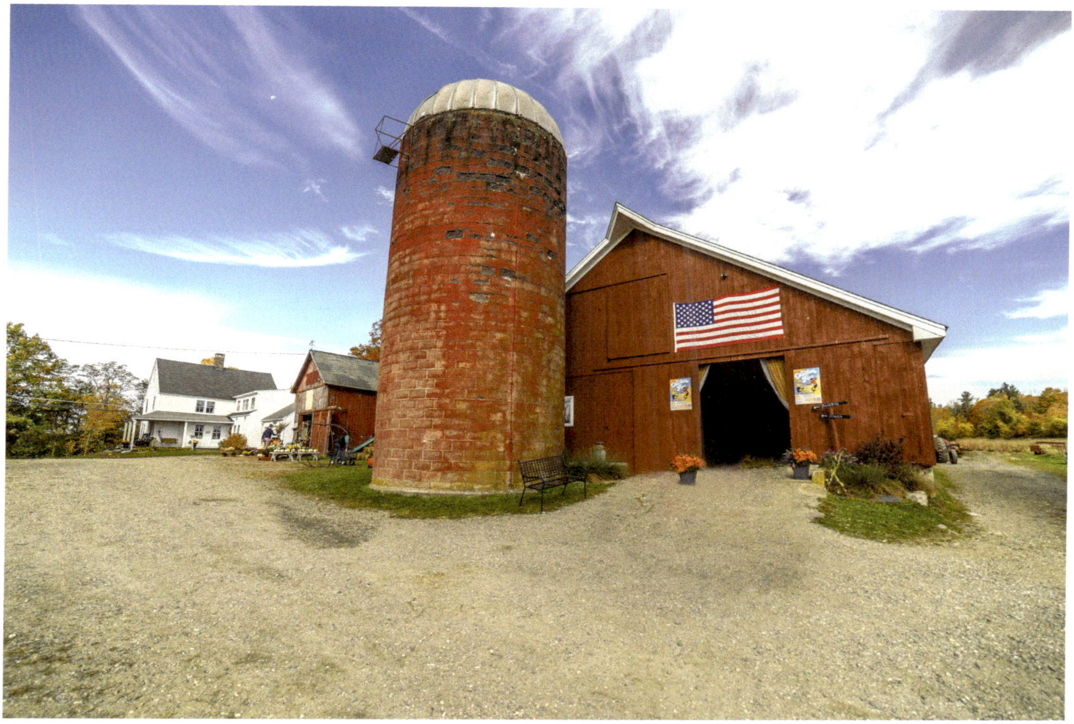

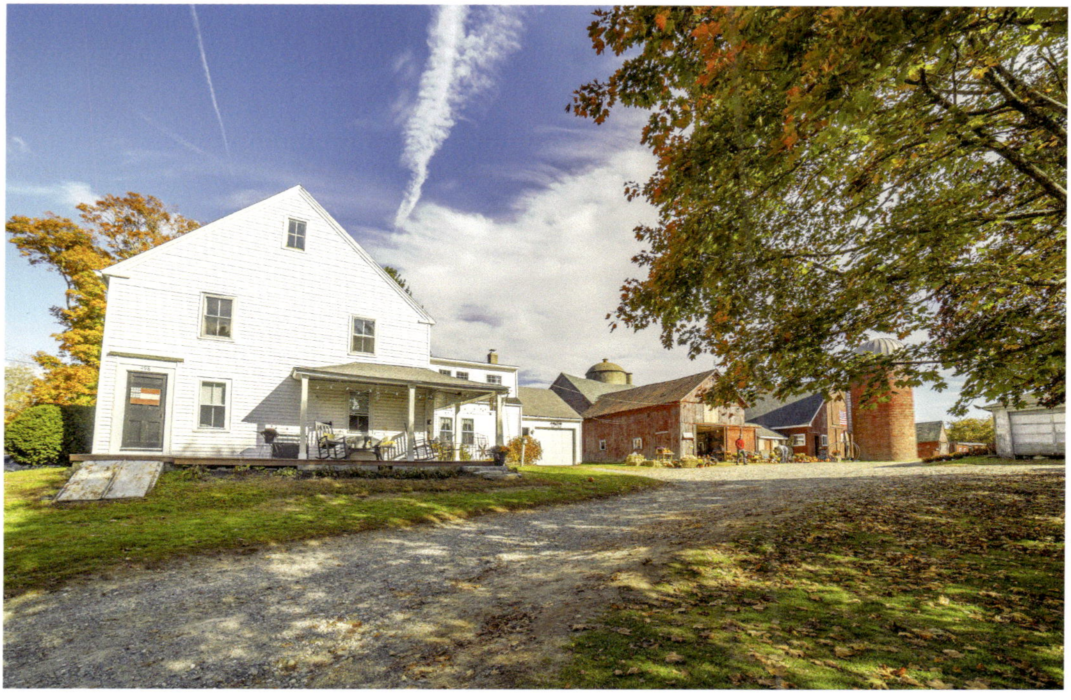

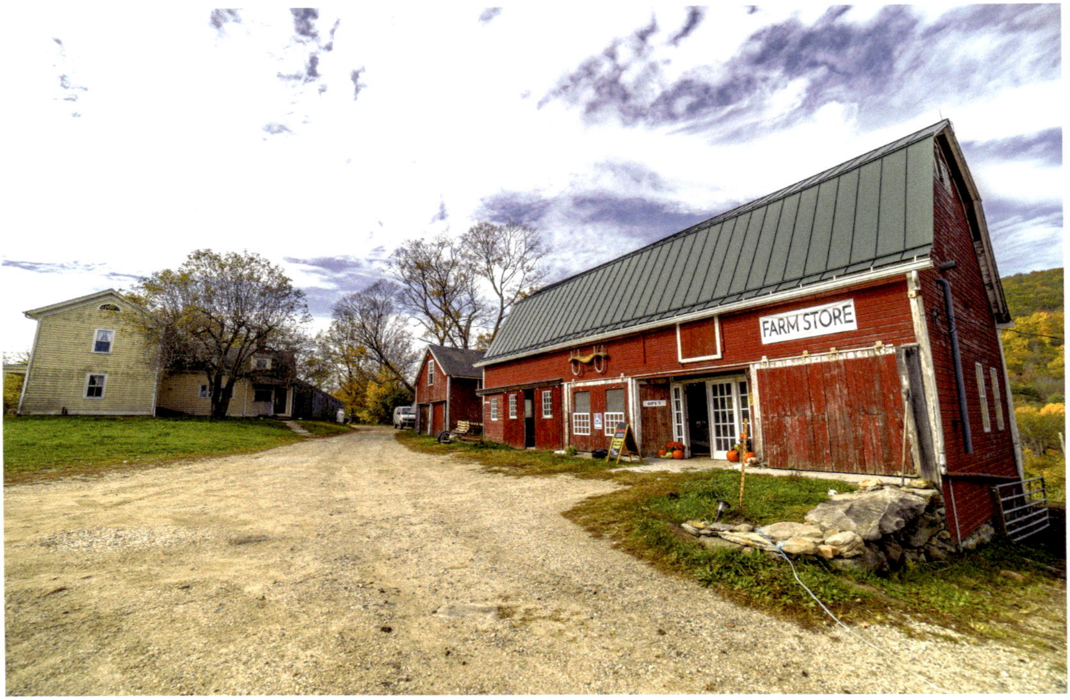

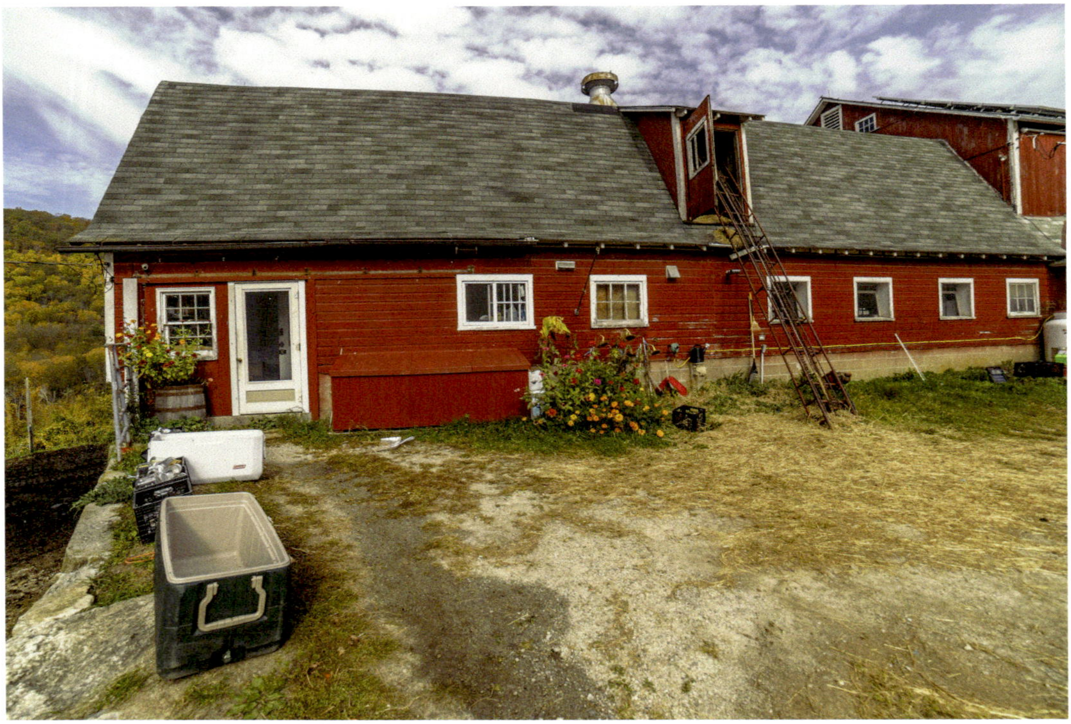

Arethusa Farm, Litchfield

I have never been an ice cream fan. I did not care for it until Arethusa came into my life. I have not found a flavor I dislike. Arethusa is divine heaven on a spoon. Three hundred cows roam the land of a farm born in 1868 and reborn in 1999 to bring us the best ice cream ever made. I say this with confidence. The only thing better is their eggnog. This family has opened three locations dedicated to "milk like it used to taste" in their unusually delectable ice cream. Starting with a small dairy plant established in a historic Bantam firehouse, Arethusa found lines of people down the sidewalk before the doors opened. They now have a New Haven and Hartford Center location, an award-winning restaurant, Arethusa al Tavolo, and a bakery, Arethusa a Mano. Arethusa's name originated after a small pink orchid growing in a swamp on the property, which seems only appropriate as Arethusa is sublime.

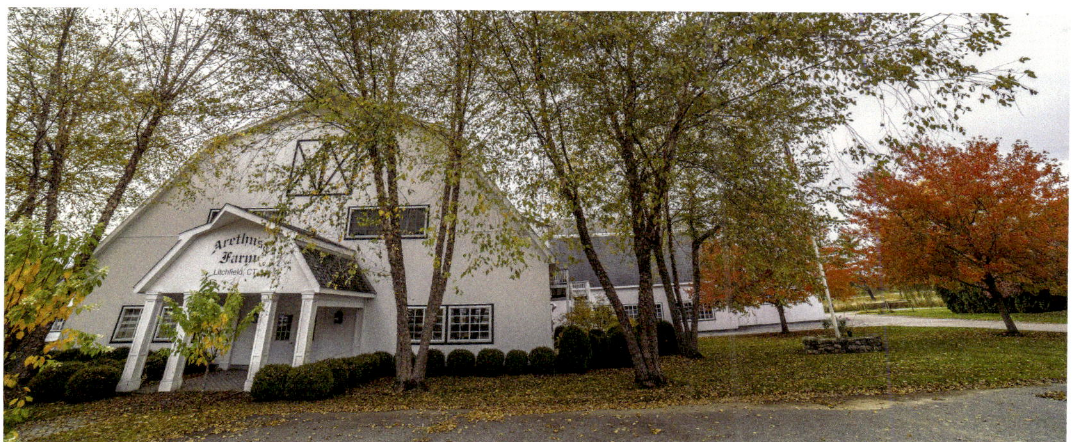

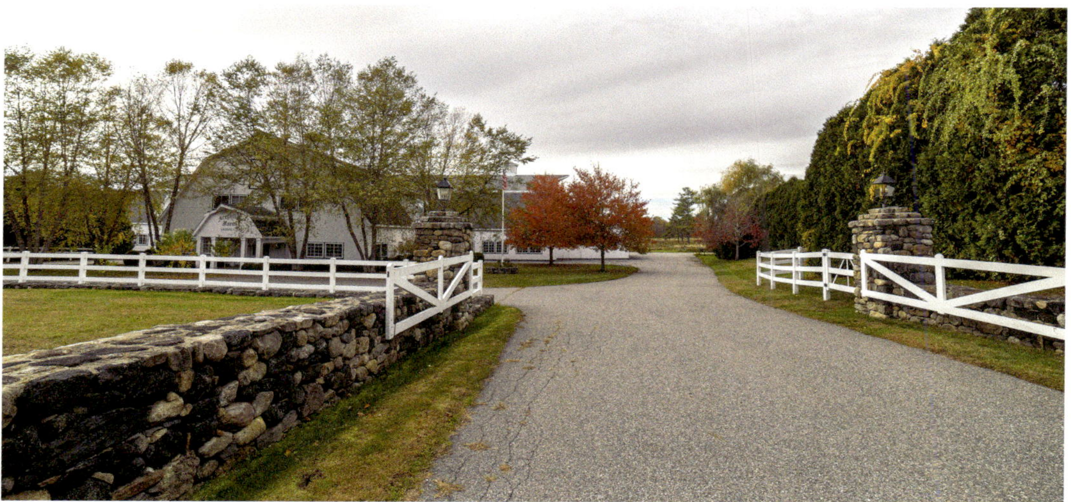

Long Ridge Farm, Litchfield

The permanently closed Long Ridge Farm in Litchfield, CT, was once on the market for a staggering $2,513,900, which translates to only $22,602 monthly for your mortgage. It has seven bathrooms, three bedrooms, with 5,362 square feet, in addition to notable agricultural barns with a silo on ninety acres. Scores of meadows, ATV trails, chicken coops, fruit trees, and blueberry crops surround the professional, tight landscaping. It is a dream anyone who wanted to start a farm couldn't fathom. To own this piece of history, you'd have to have Millennial or Gen Z jobs chasing butterflies and raising Gila monsters for twenty-seven hours a week. All joking aside, Long Ridge Farm had provided dairy and beef cattle since 1998 before closing.

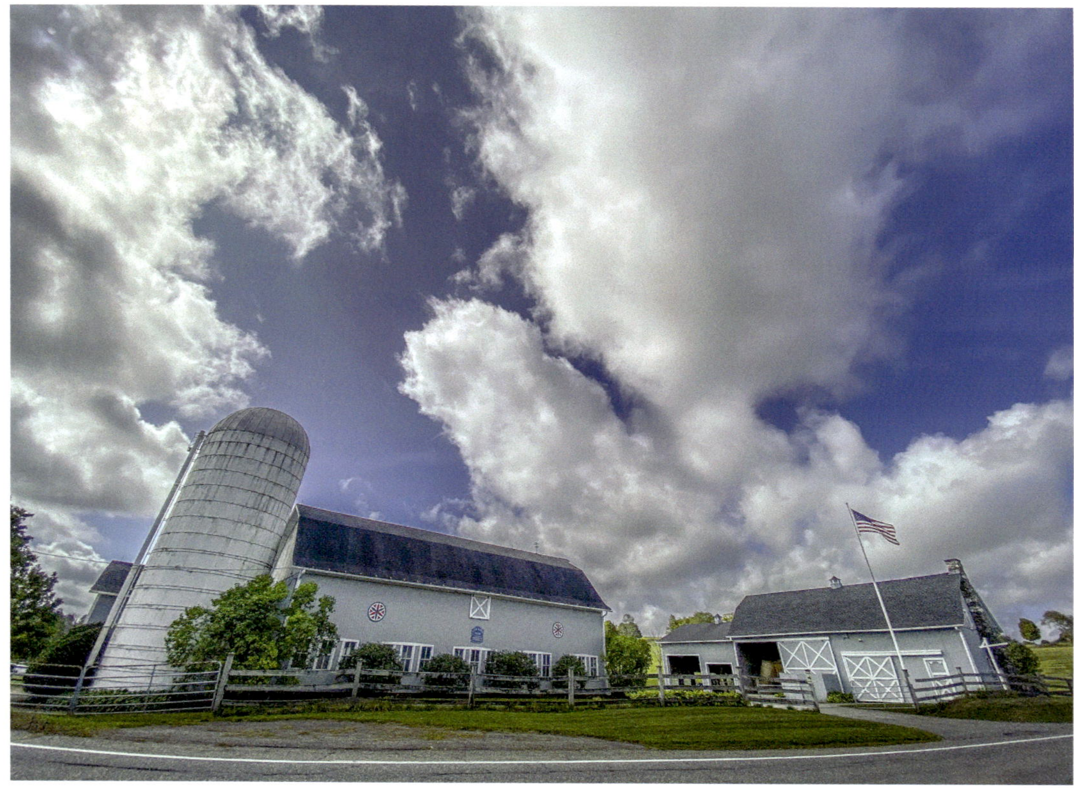

13

New Canaan and Wilton

Grace Farms

Grace Farms River building is the foundation's center. The epitome of farm evolution, Grace Farms is a hub for collaboration to push its agenda of ending modern slavery and implementing more grace and compassion in a peaceful setting. The farm focuses on the arts, education, nature, justice, community, and faith with a design for freedom.

Weir Farm, Wilton

Weir Farms is a National Park for Art. The structures on this art farm inspired impressionist J. Alden Weir to have his home and studios on the painterly sixty acres. In 1883, Weir made Branchville Farm his home for thirty-six years. The farm often hosted "the Ten." The Ten consisted of ten American painters: William Merritt Chase, Frank W. Benson, Edmund Tarbell, Thomas W. Dewing, Joseph DeCamp, Edward Simmons, Willard Metcalf, Childe Hassam, Julian Alden Weir, and Robert Reid. Honorable mention to acclaimed artist John Singer Sargent, a frequent visitor. The farm still hosts artists' retreats, competitions, children's activities, and workshops, and it is open daily, from sunrise to sunset, year-round.

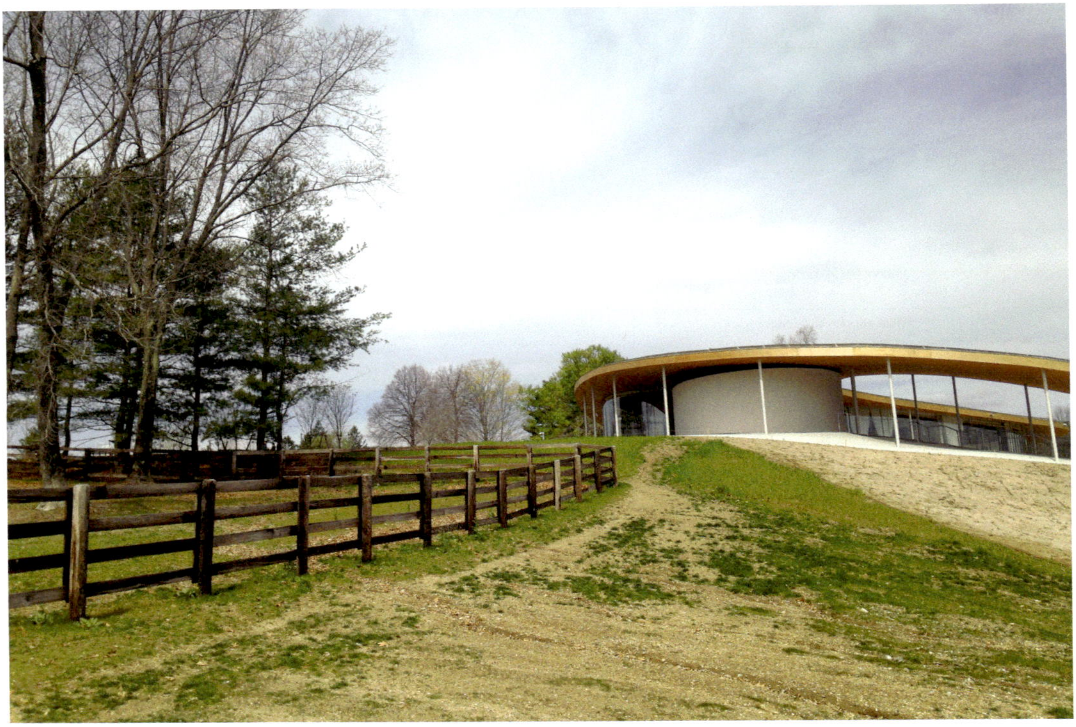

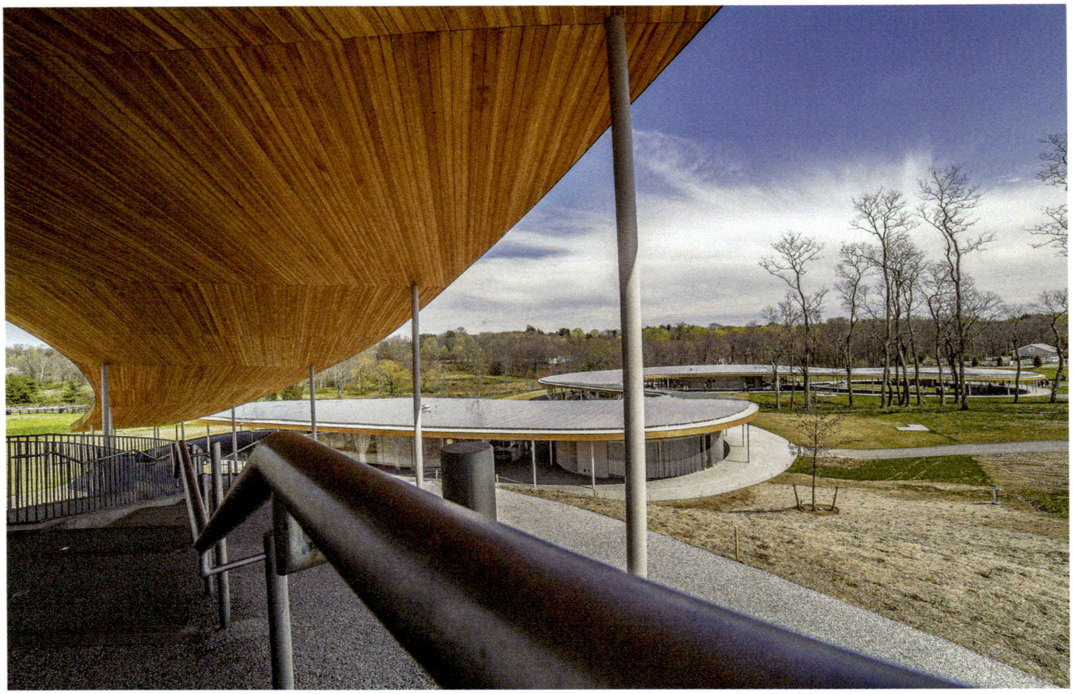

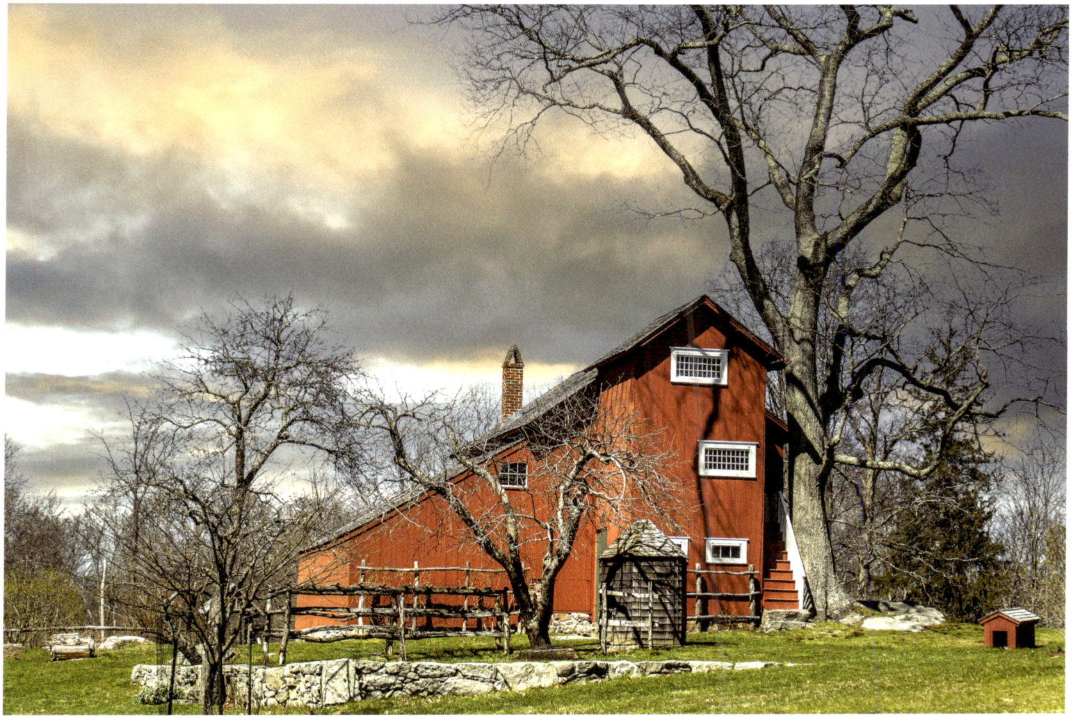

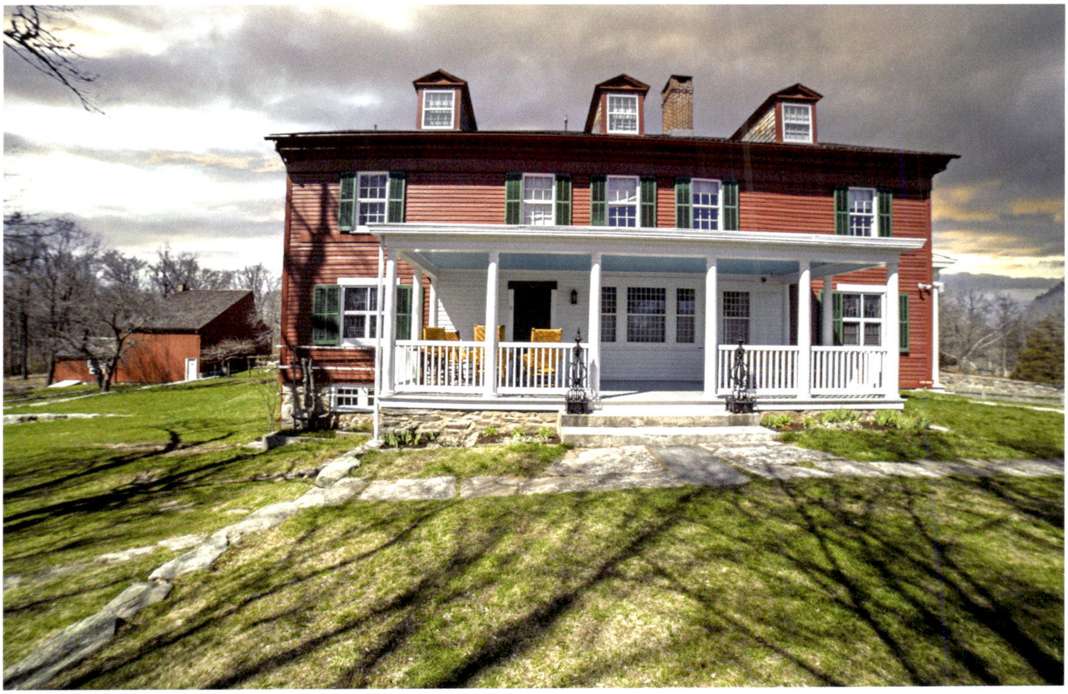

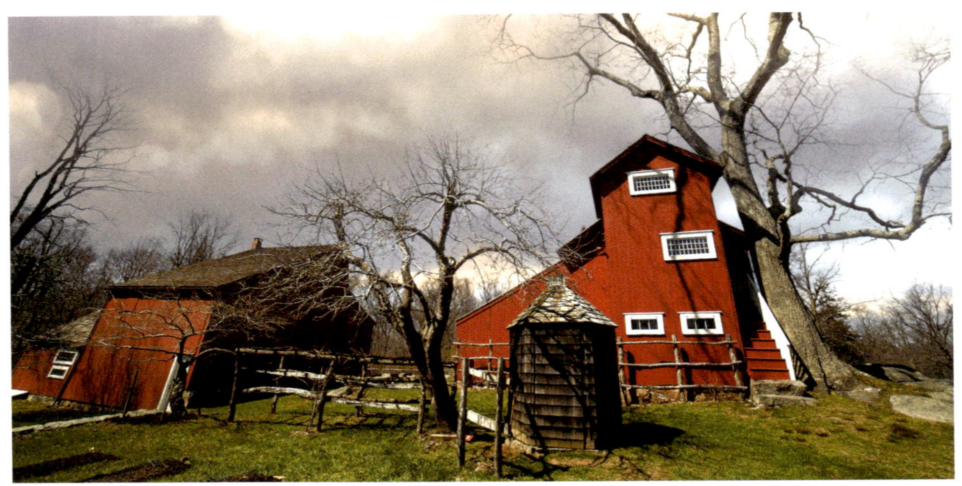

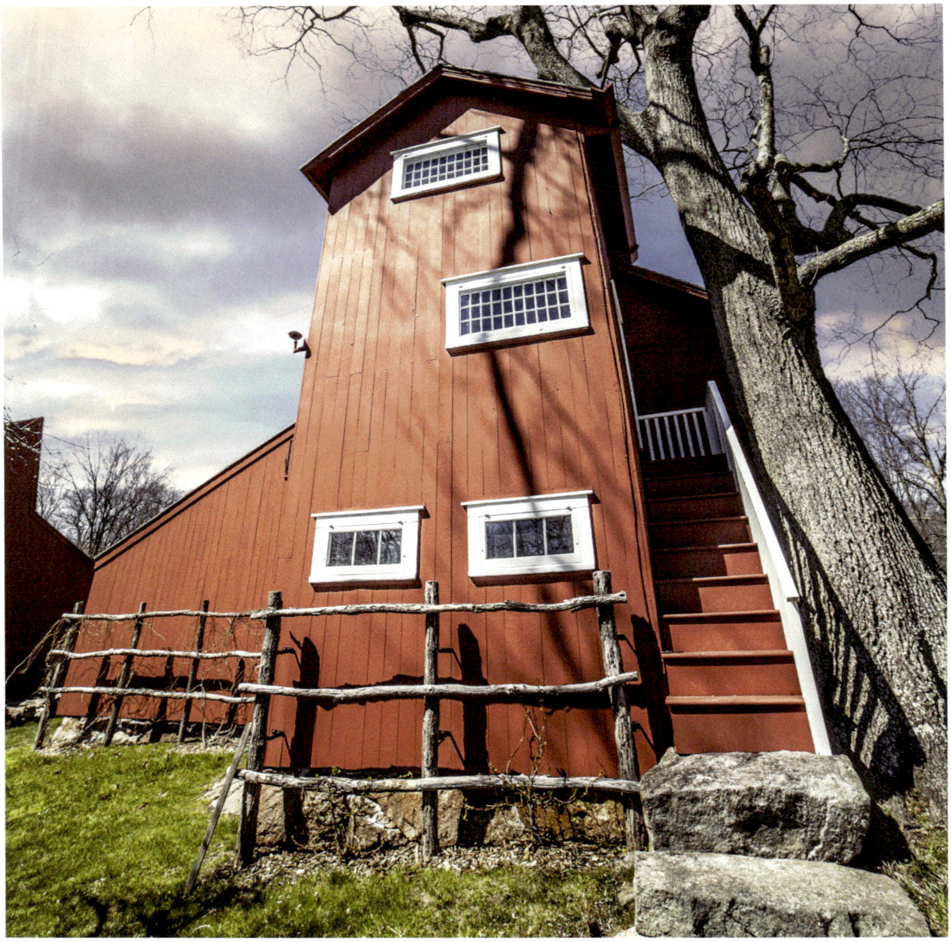

14

Sunflower Farms

Buttonwood Sunflower Farms, Griswold

Buttonwood has been growing sunflowers for a good cause since 1975. Buttonwood started as a dairy farm, and sunflower crops became a reality shcrtly after. It was born from the lumber of their land. Dairy and beef cattle birthed their next step: the inception and building of their ice cream stand. The goals of maintaining their agricultural landscape, fulfilled by sunflowers accenting the stone walls and pastoral fields, stretch as far as the eye can see. The ice, whipped cream, and waffle cones are handmade, and taste every bit of the love put into them. By far, Buttonwood is my second favorite ice cream ever. Connecticut certainly taught me one thing, and that was what good ice cream is. Proceeds from the Buttonwood Sunflowers have often gone to the Connecticut Make-a-Wish Foundation.

Sunflower Fields of North Brandford

The Auger Farm has housed a sea of sunflowers for locals and passersby for years. Rumor has it that when Larry Augur passed in 2016, his beloved continued to grow them in his honor until today. The story was more romanticized when I heard it initially, stating that the sunflower field was grown by a lovelorn farmer who lost his wife in a tragic accident. He plants the field of happiness, adding a new yearly row in her memory. Locals and tourists alike enjoy the seas of yellow in the summer days. The family of Larry and his wife continue his excellent work. High schoolers have come to Auger Farm to maintain plots, grow food, and learn about a working farm. The sunflower visits are still free and a continual draw for the community. Walk amongst the bees and hummingbirds through the rows; shutterbugs are invited!

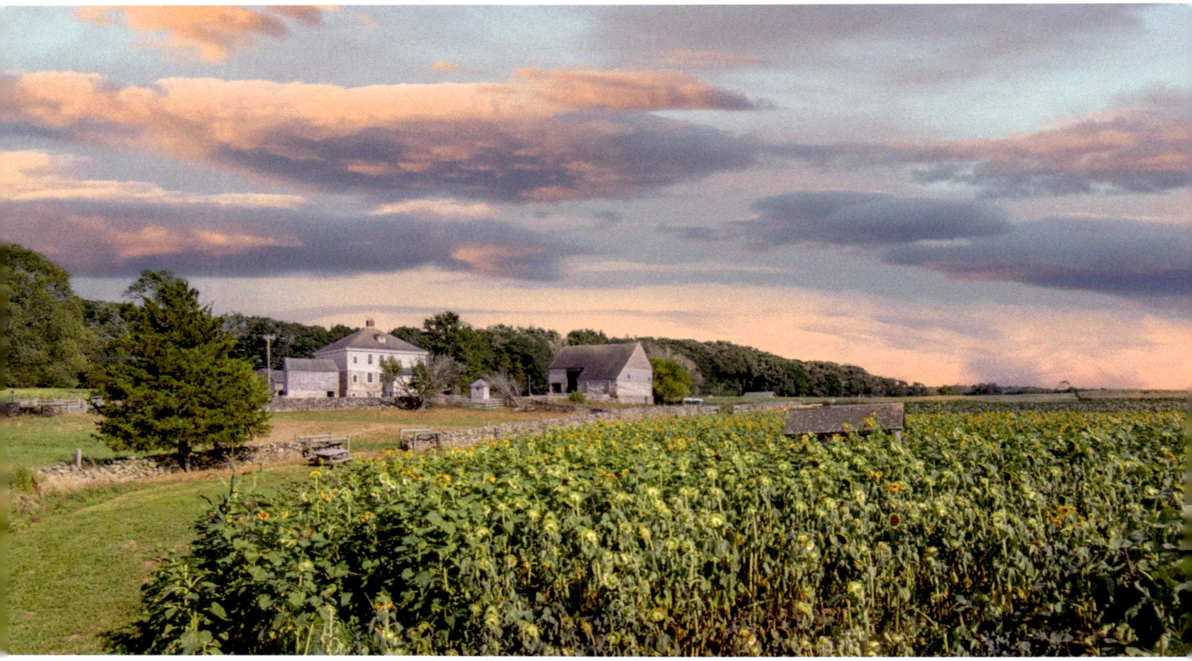

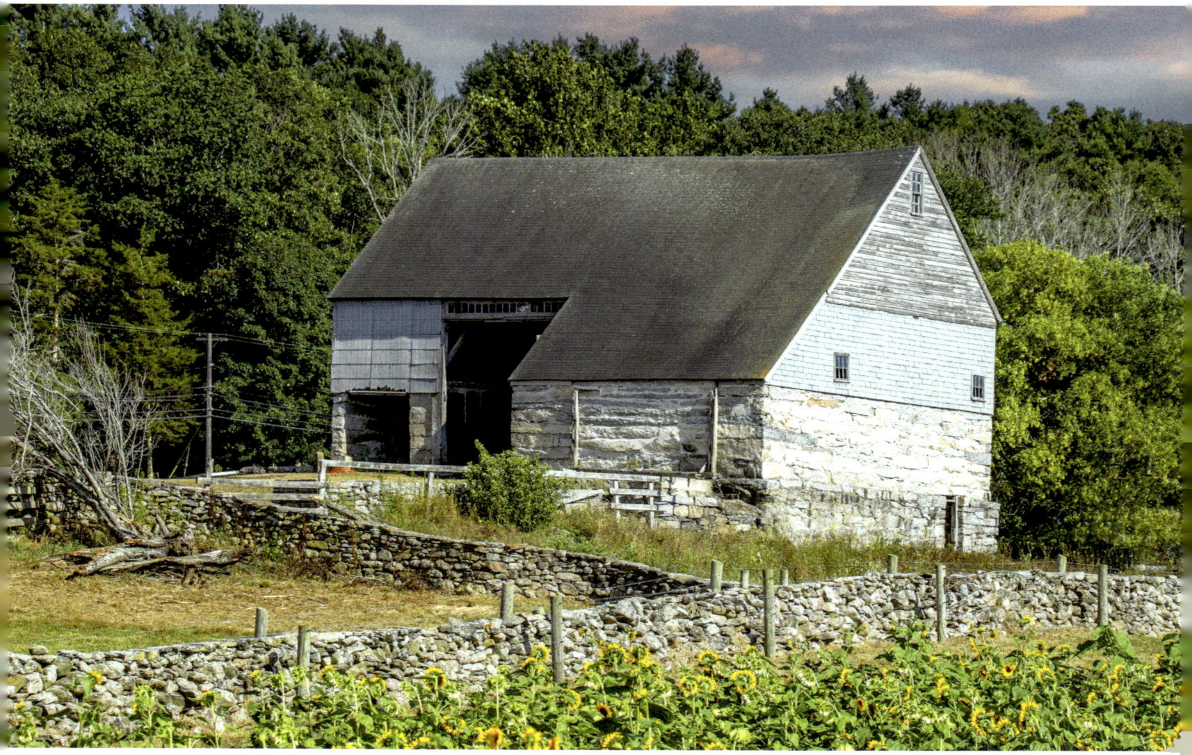

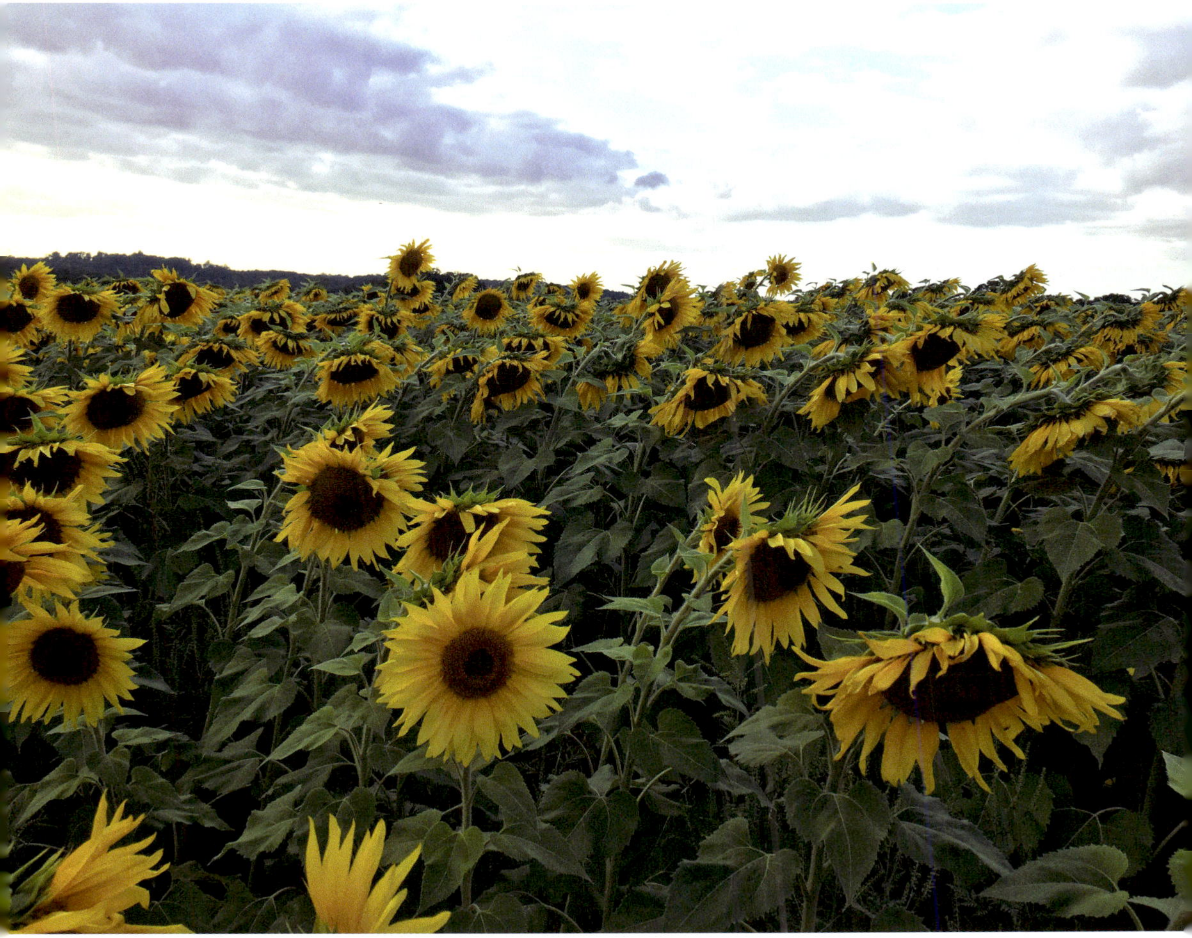

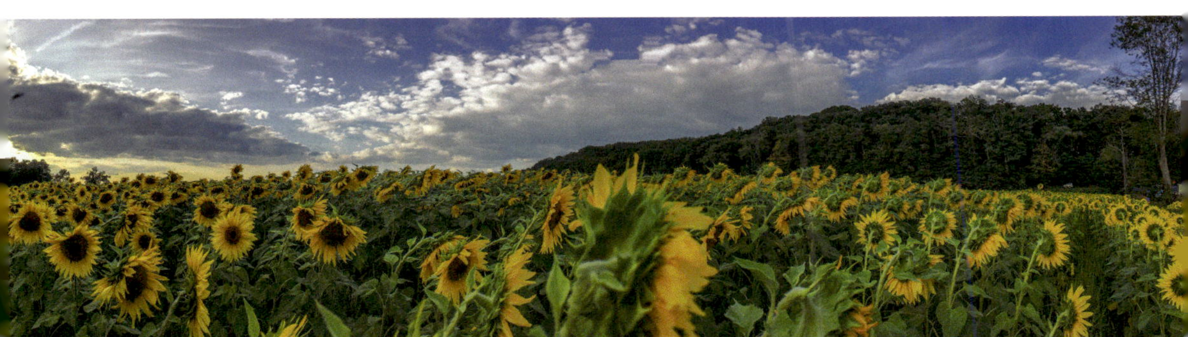

15

Fancy Farm Stands and Attractions

Beaumont Farms

Beaumont Farms is always a pleaser. Christmas attractions that channel Clark Griswold and *National Lampoon's Christmas Vacation* to Sweet Easter setups of Candyland and Peanuts to make children squeal in a magical dreamland. Beaumont caters to their customers' imaginations and their vegetable and nursery needs. Beaumont's farm stand is a gorgeous example of what one can do with a little stand and some design savvy. The stand is a Mother's Day lifesaver as any passersby can pull up on the curb and get a quick bouquet. Displays appear on holidays at the corner of East Center Street and Airline Road. However, October of 2023 brought a catastrophe when Billy Beaumont, everyone's favorite farmer, suffered severe burns at the hands of a freak accident. We anxiously await to see if Billy will do more larger-than-life displays or need more time to heal. Whatever happens, all appreciate Billy and his fantastic ideas, and the state awaits when he will return.

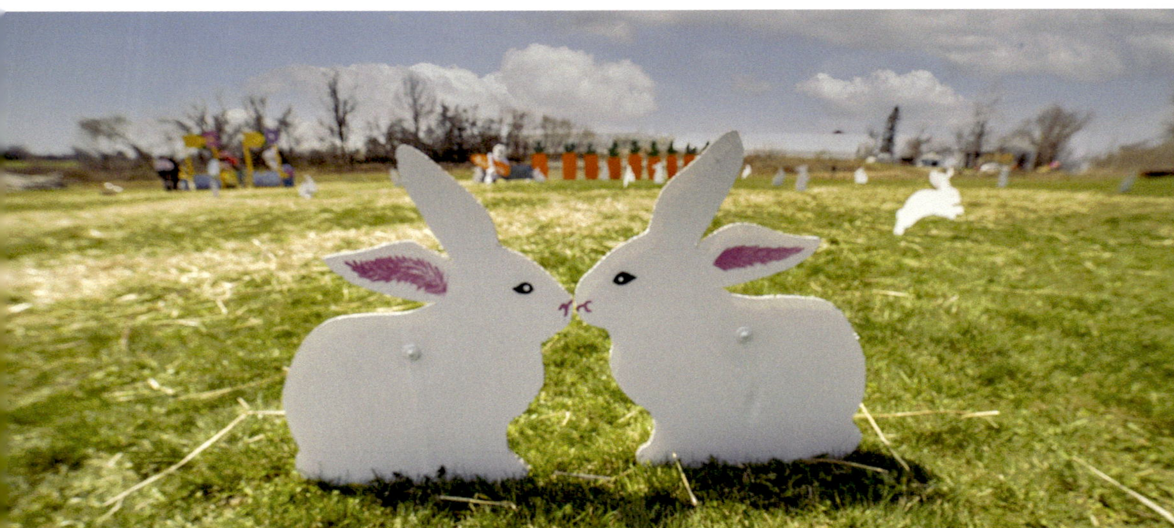

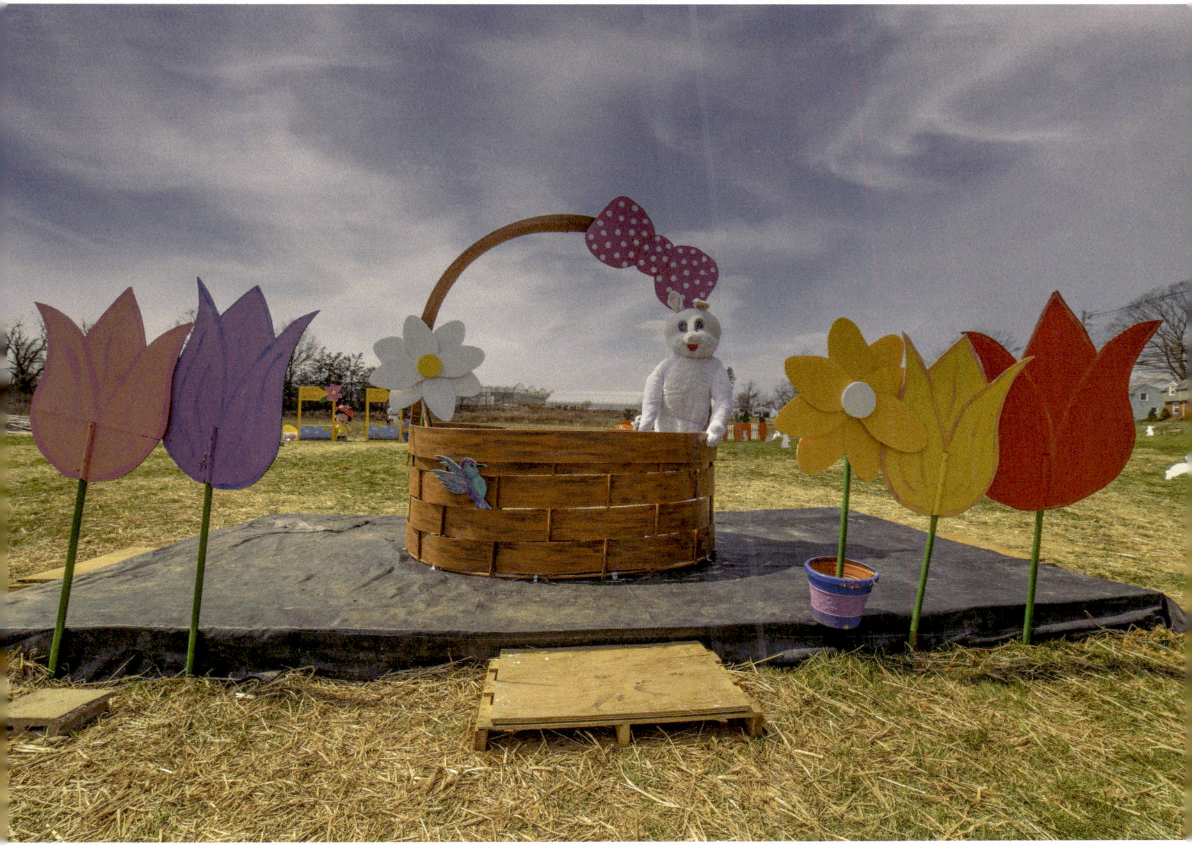

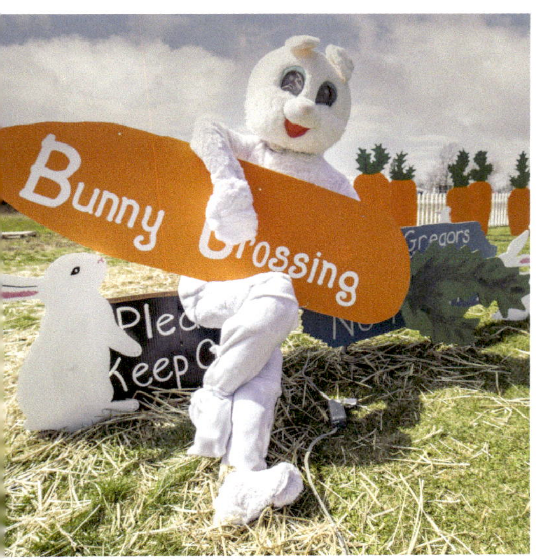
Bunny Crossing
Plea
Keep C
Gregors
NO

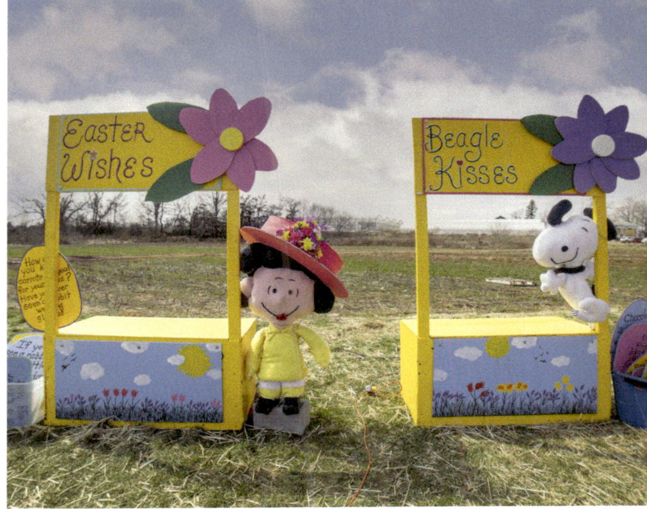
Easter
Wishes
Beagle
Kisses

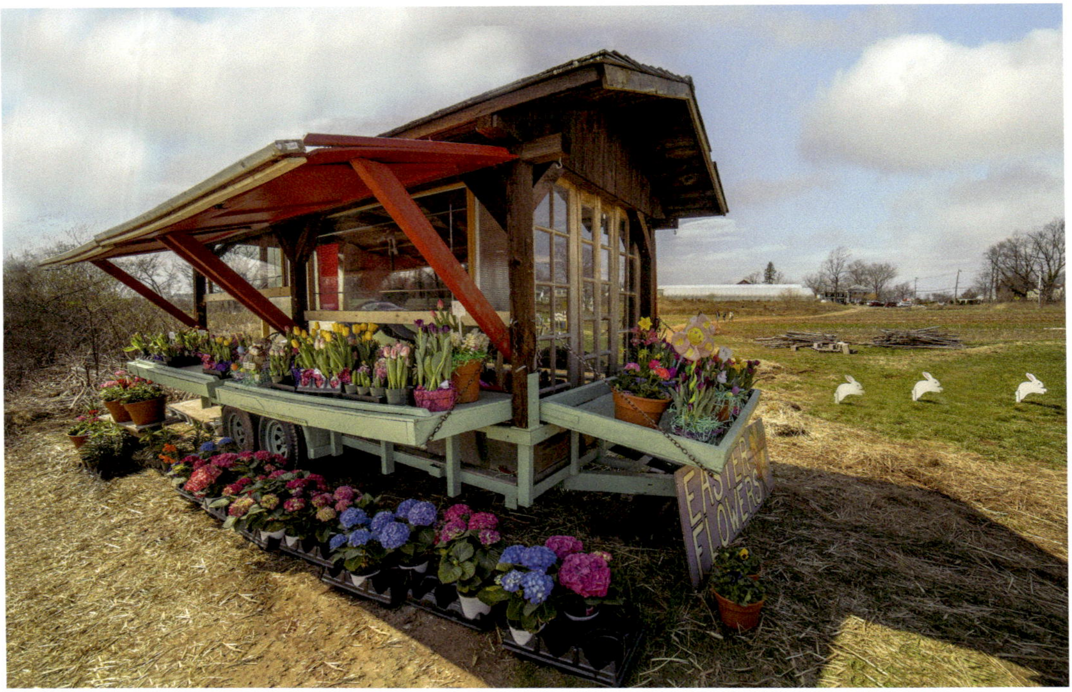

EASTER
FLOWERS

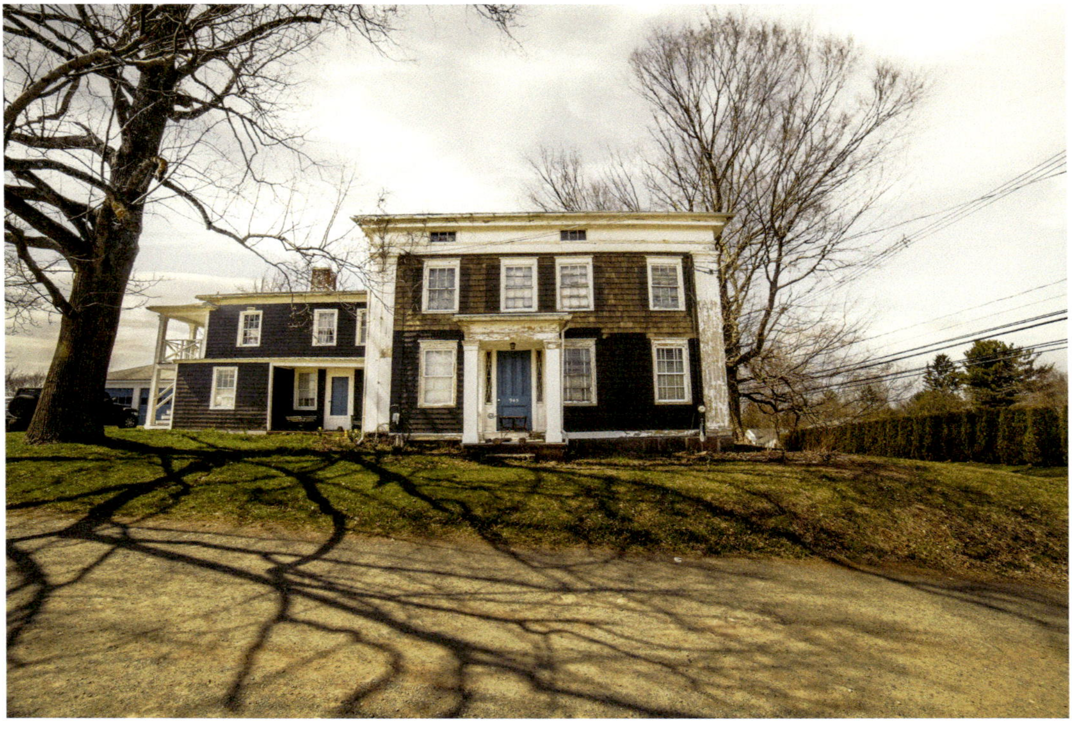

Farmington

Farmington is home to Hein Farm and the Farmington Farm Truck. Their season starts in March, and they offer CSA membership and the state's only mobile farm stand. The mobile farm stand features many different farmers' produce and farm-made products and acts as a fully functioning farmer's market. The truck is available for events or visiting businesses. When on the grounds, people can cut their flower bouquets, visit the rustic barn shop full of goodies, or buy numerous vegetation types from the greenhouses and grounds. In addition to making us healthy with their organically grown and raised items, Hein Farm is big on giving back. Concerts are held on the property to raise money for local youth sports teams, scholarships are given to local students interested in agriculture, and food is donated to the food pantry.

On the corner of Red Oak Hill and Meadow Road, Mt. View Farm Stand and Coffee Shop offers native veggies, but one can grab a cup of coffee and enjoy the atmosphere. The rustic little barn provides the quaintness of hand-painted signs and cheery vibes. The original farm originated in 1921 and offers multiple farm stands where you can discover their deliciousness. Sweet corn and peaches are the brag-about crops being brought to us by three generations of Mt. View's farmers.

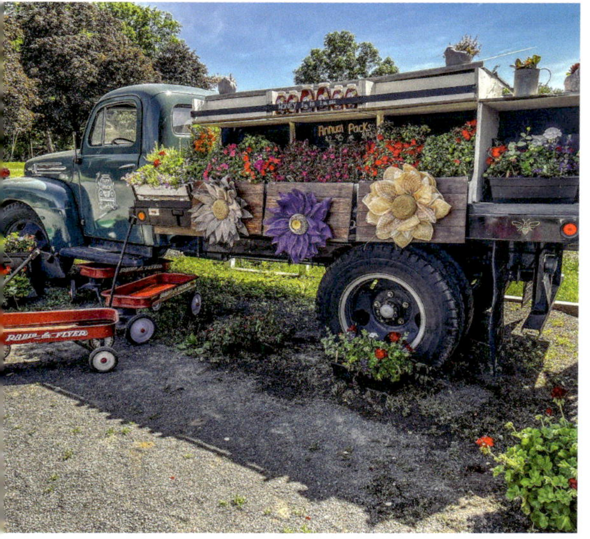

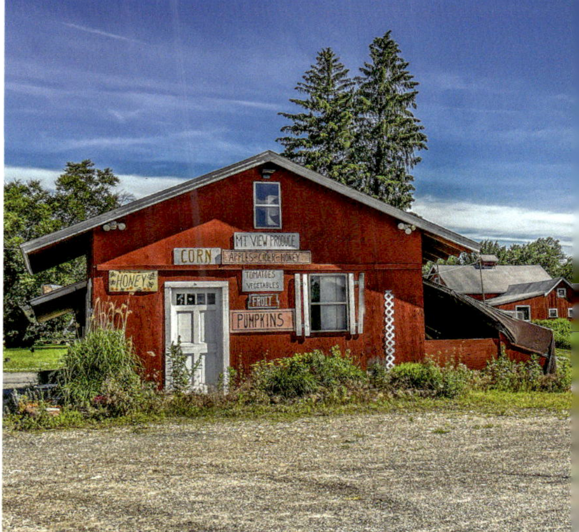

16

George Hendee Farm, aka Hill Top, Suffield

This historic 1913 farm, incited as a Gentleman's Retirement Farm, was the creation of George Hendee, Indian Motorcycles' co-founder. A large community garden serves the locality for budding flowers and producing farmers. The big white barn and acreage are run by the Friends of the Farm at Hilltop (FOFAH), who have maintained the property since 2003. Sixty of the acres of land for conservation is leased to the town, and upkeep involves all structures on the eleven acres where the buildings sit. Taking the paths toward the river, one can see nesting bald eagles and rarities such as the red-headed woodpecker. The Audubon's bird count considers this area a hotspot for birders. High school work days, yoga, and children's programs are just some of the features Hill Top offers the public.

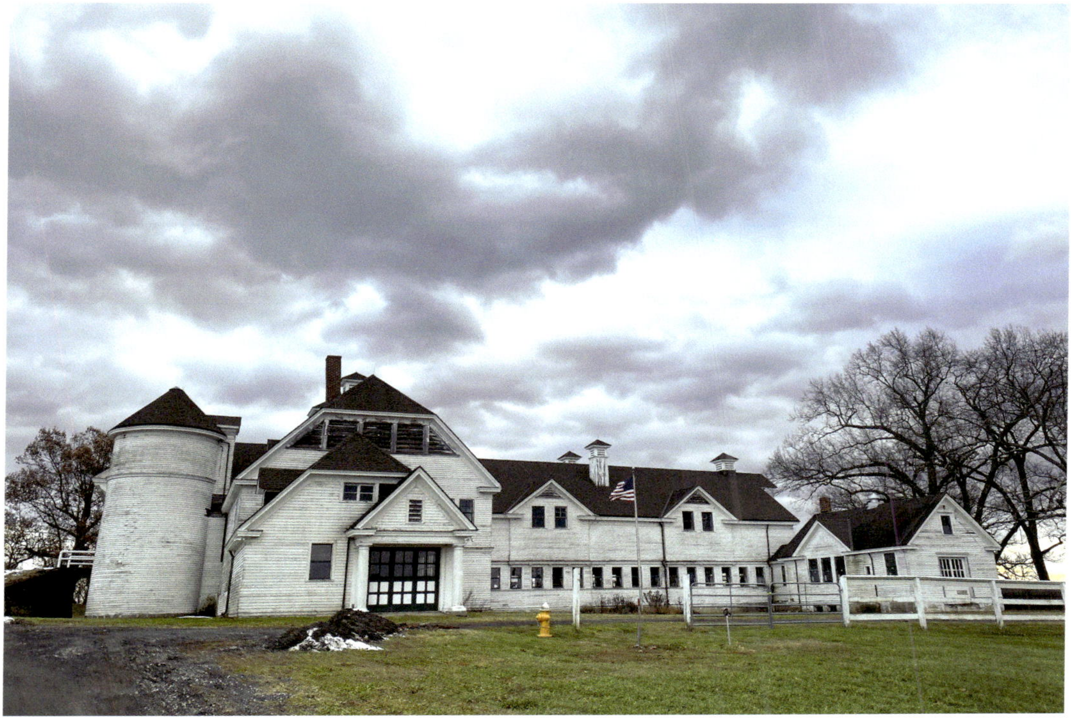

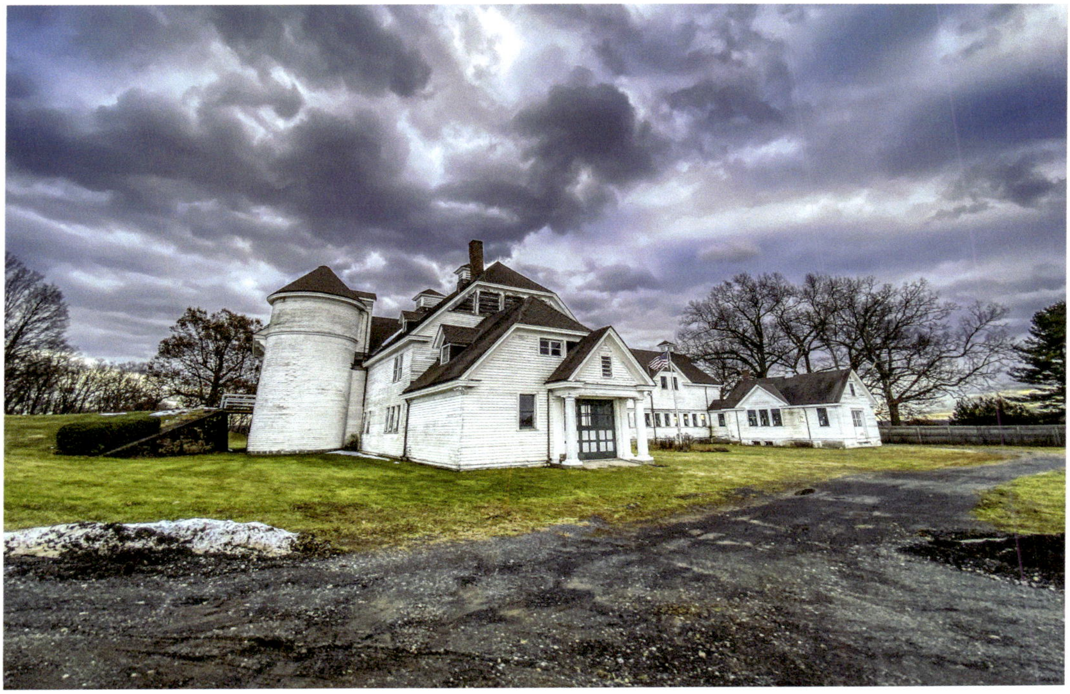

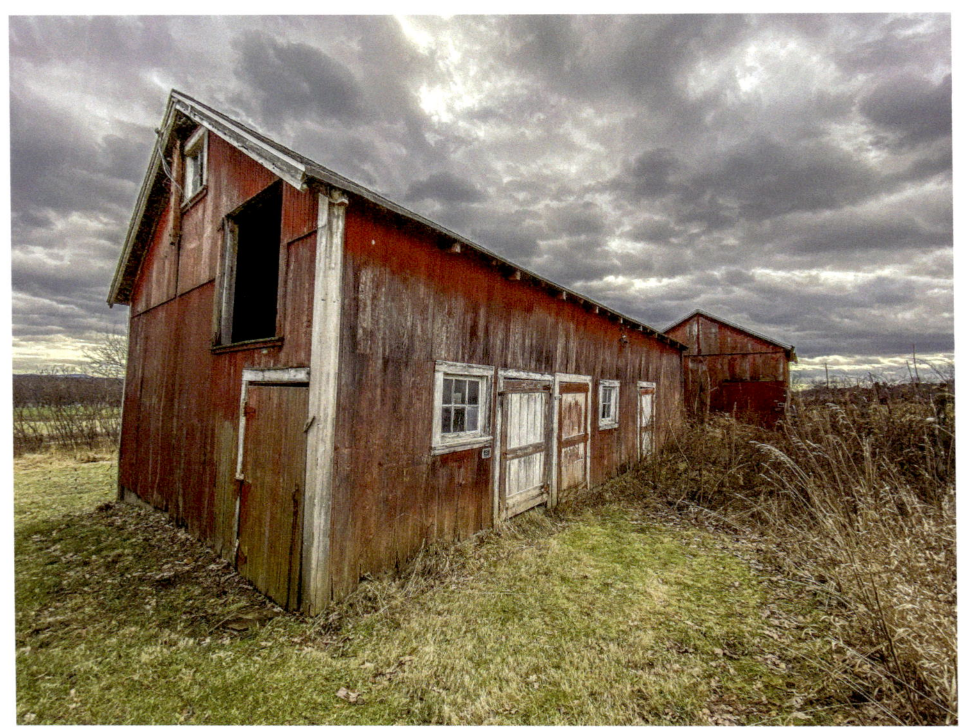

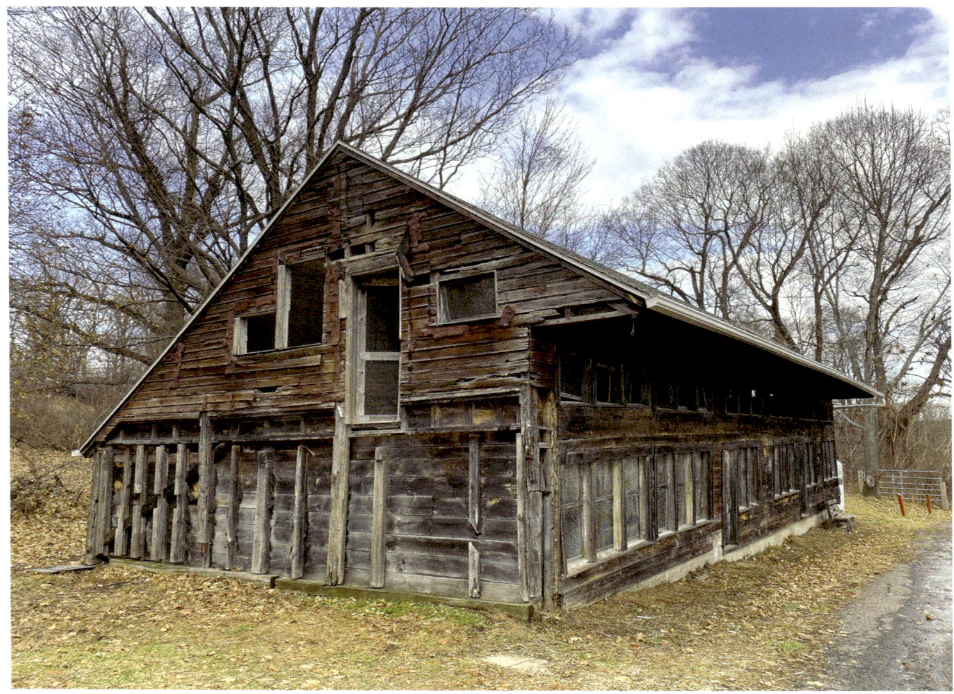

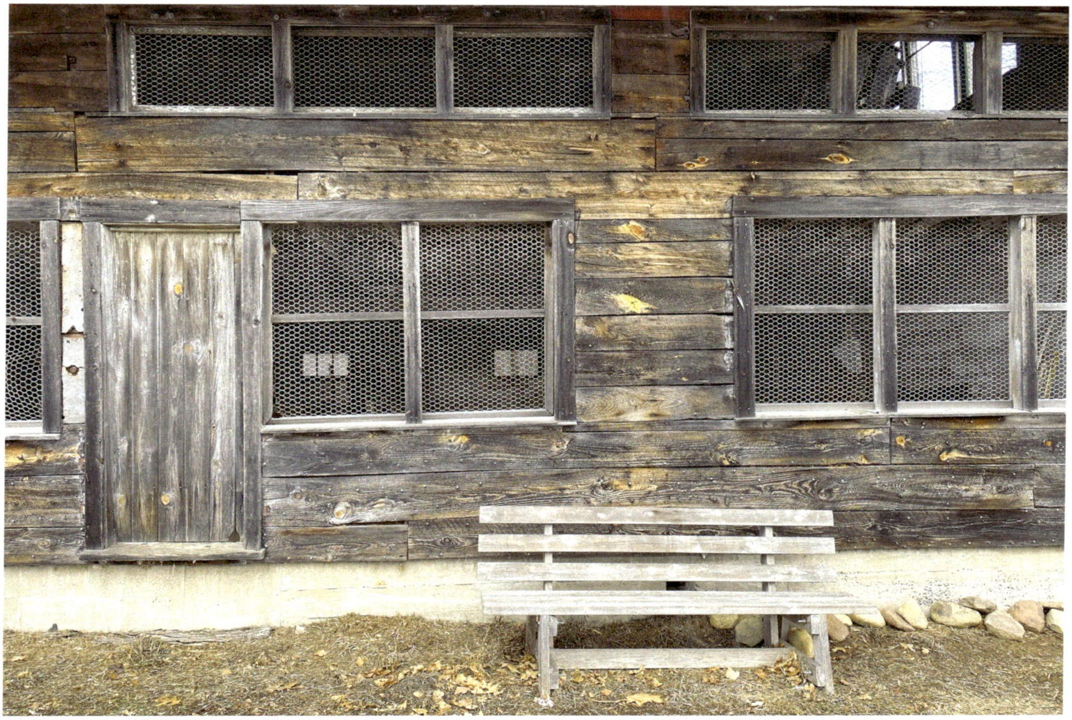

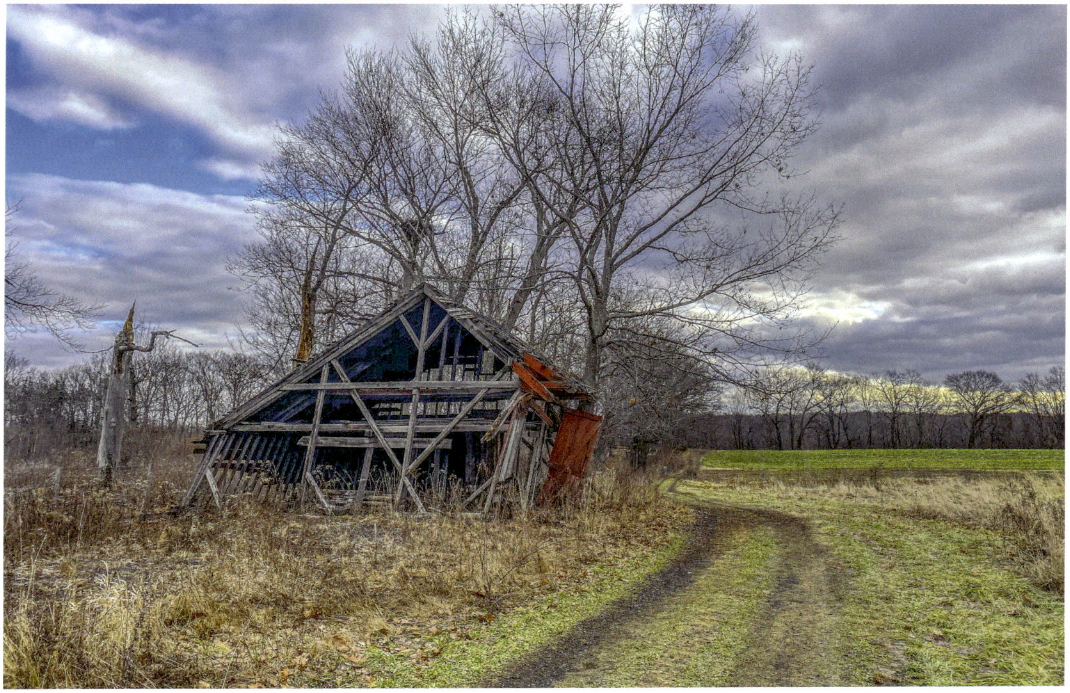

Middlefield Barn

Along the Connecticut Barn Trail sits this ever-changing picturesque barn surrounded by curving roads, Lyman's Orchards, and Lyman's golf course. Yet, if you looked at and lost yourself in this structure and foliage in every season, you would not know the latter existed. If visiting, use a zoom as the owner does not favor tourist admiration.

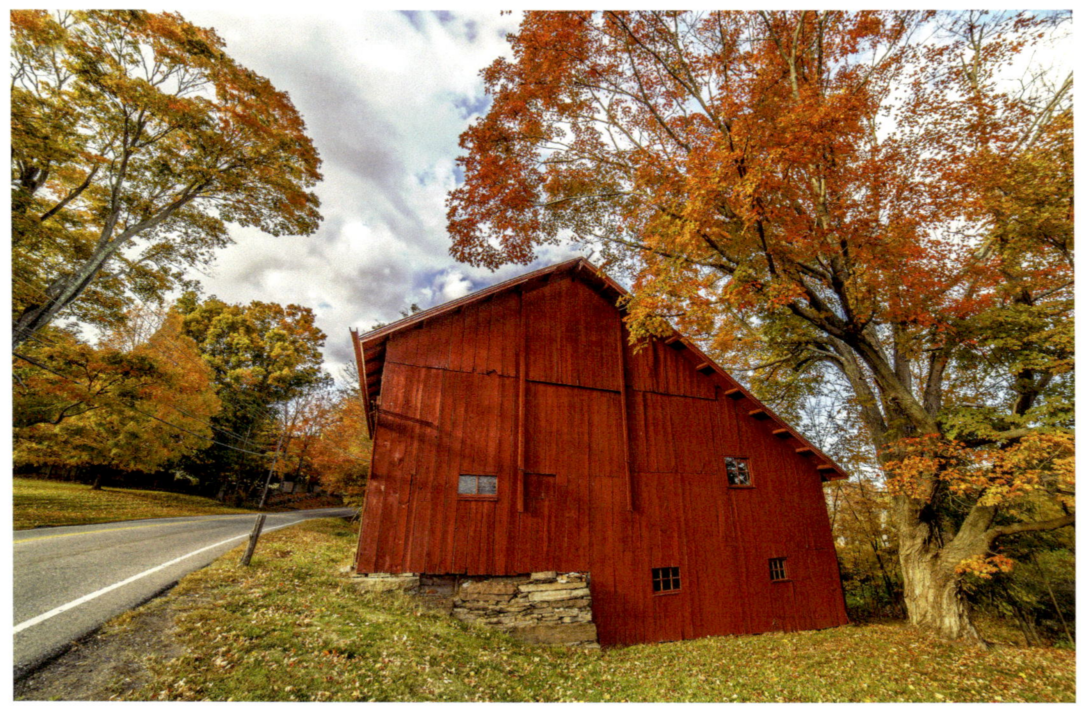

Bradley Mountain and Aussaakita Acres Socialization Farms

Many farms offer excursions that let you come, hold, cuddle, and socialize their animal babies. Bradley Mountain Farms, Southington, has baby goats that wear seasonal hats. Animal Adventures in Canterbury has a wide variety of critters for loving. Flamig Farms, West Simsbury, and many others offer Alpaca adventures, but the cuddliest are Aussaakita Acres and its adorable piglets. If piglets are not enough, baby goats are available. Aussaakita owns the goat yoga destination title.

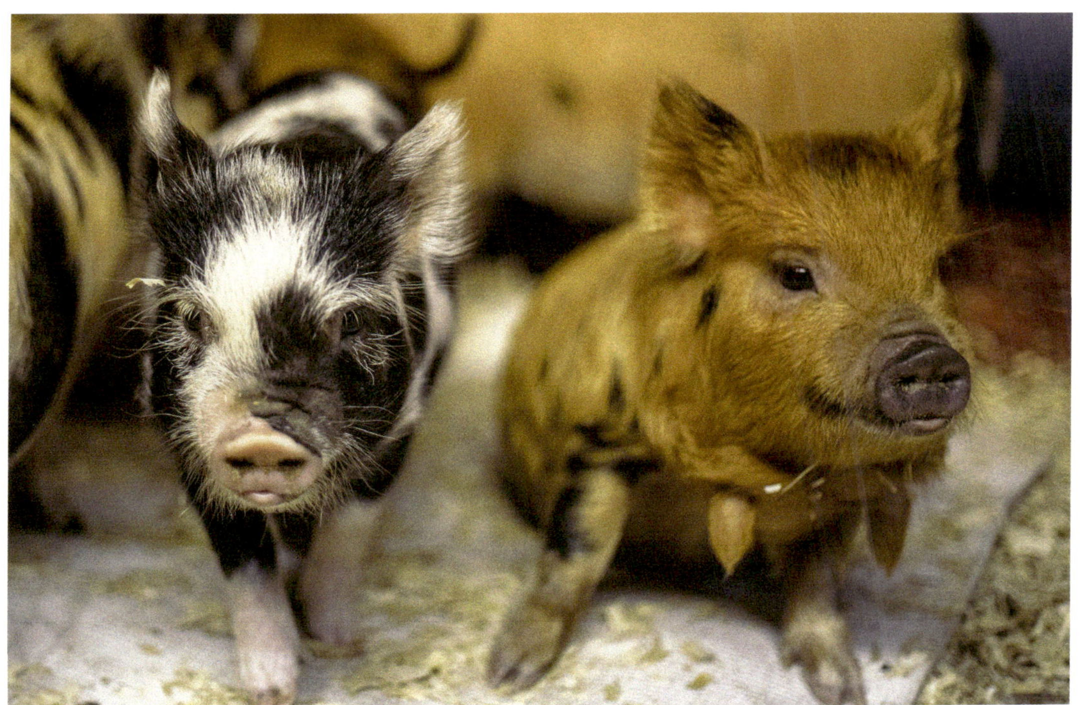

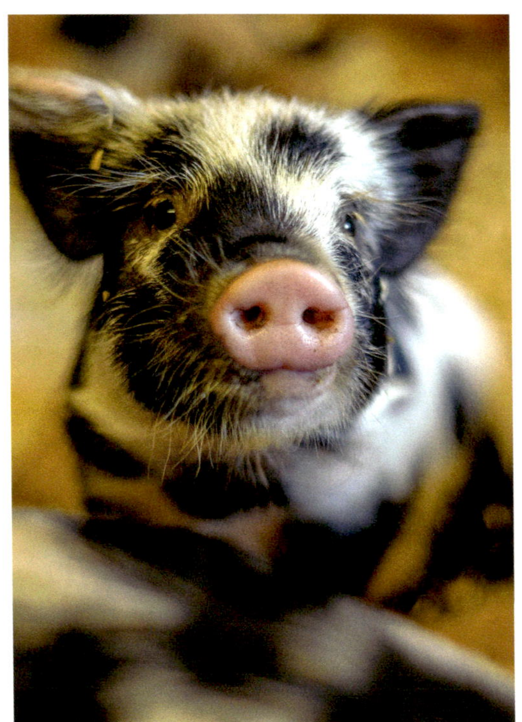
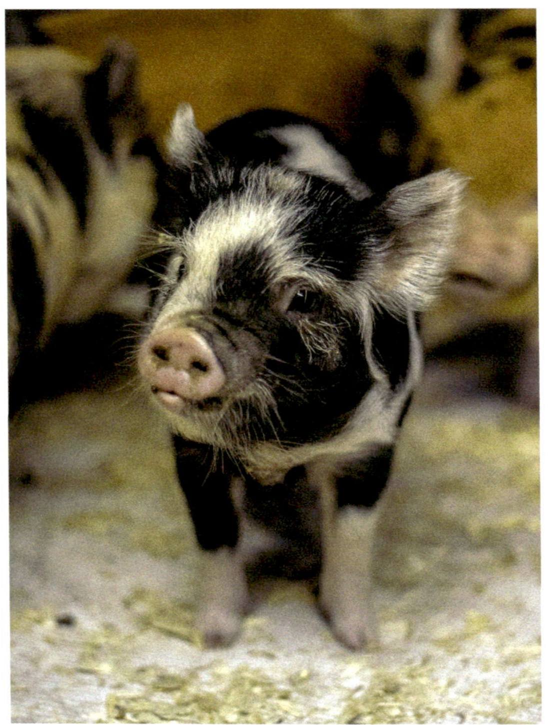

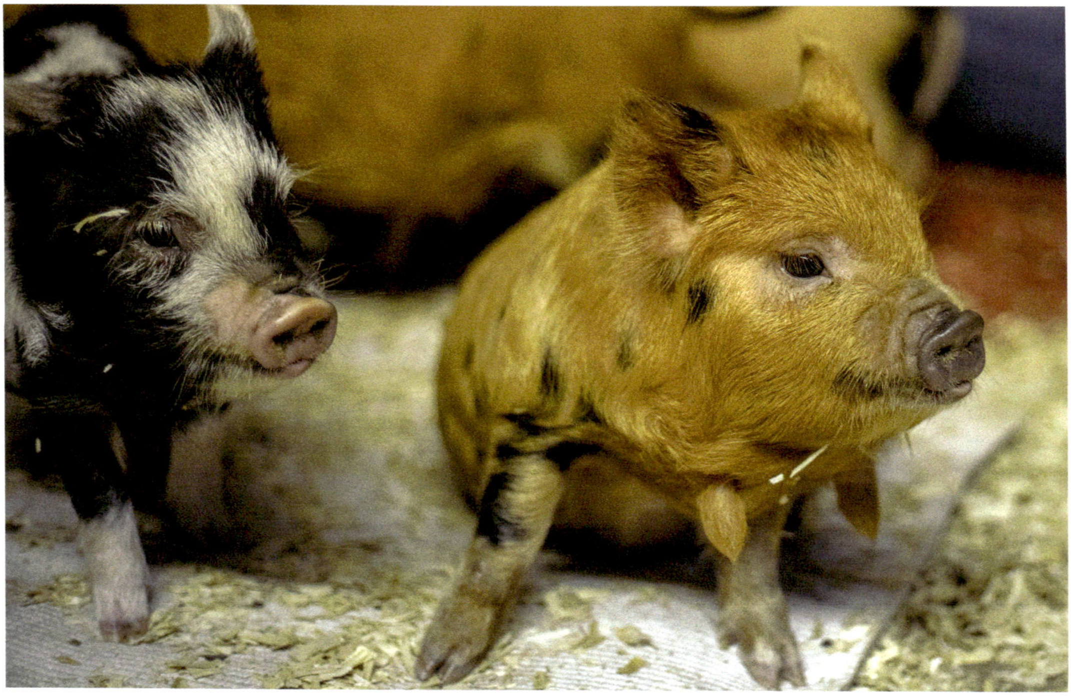

19

Tiffany Farms, Lyme

Tiffany Farms, a 1700s dairy farm, was a working farm until 2017. After the passing of Mr. Tiffany in 2018, his wife and son turned the farm into a beef farm dedicated to offering the best beef in Connecticut with their Waygu mixed stock. Tiffany added a farmer's market, offering the freshest produce and flowers from many farmers in the region. As of 2024, twelve farms are signed up for the season every Saturday, starting in May and running through October. Friendly cows and beautiful scenery make for the best pictures. Instagram is waiting!

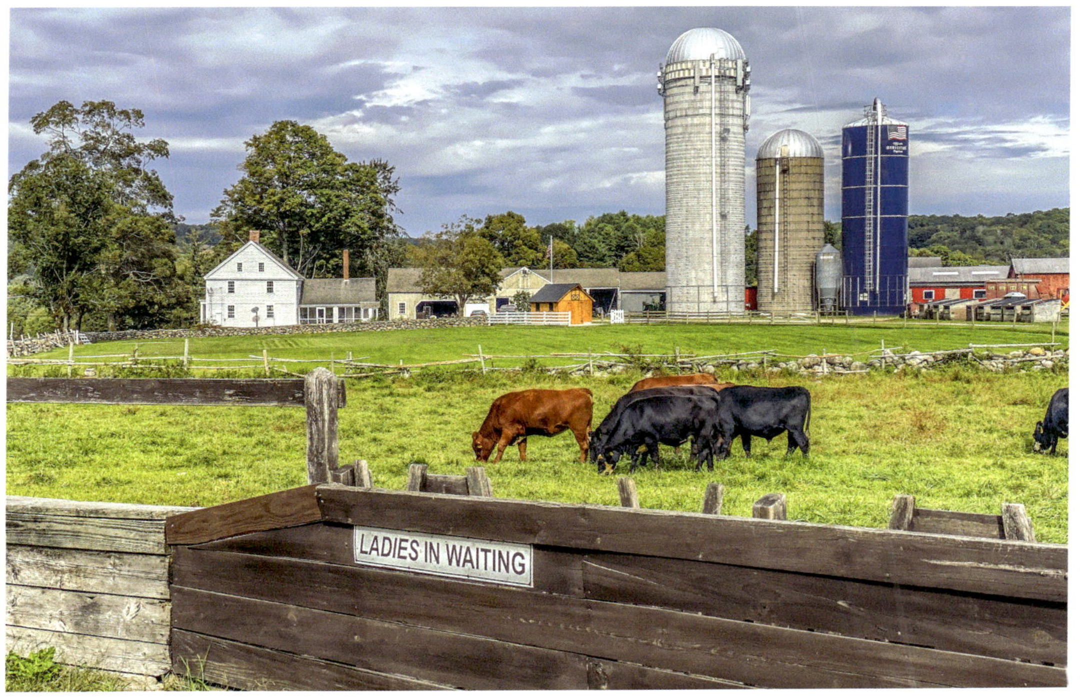

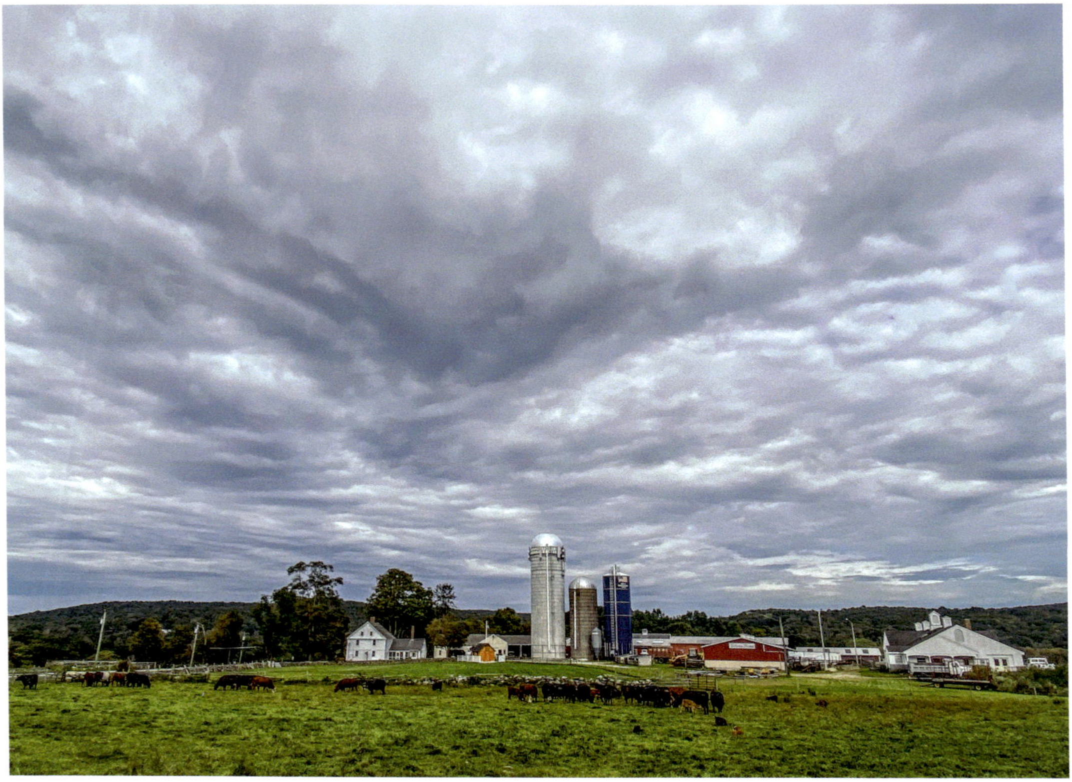

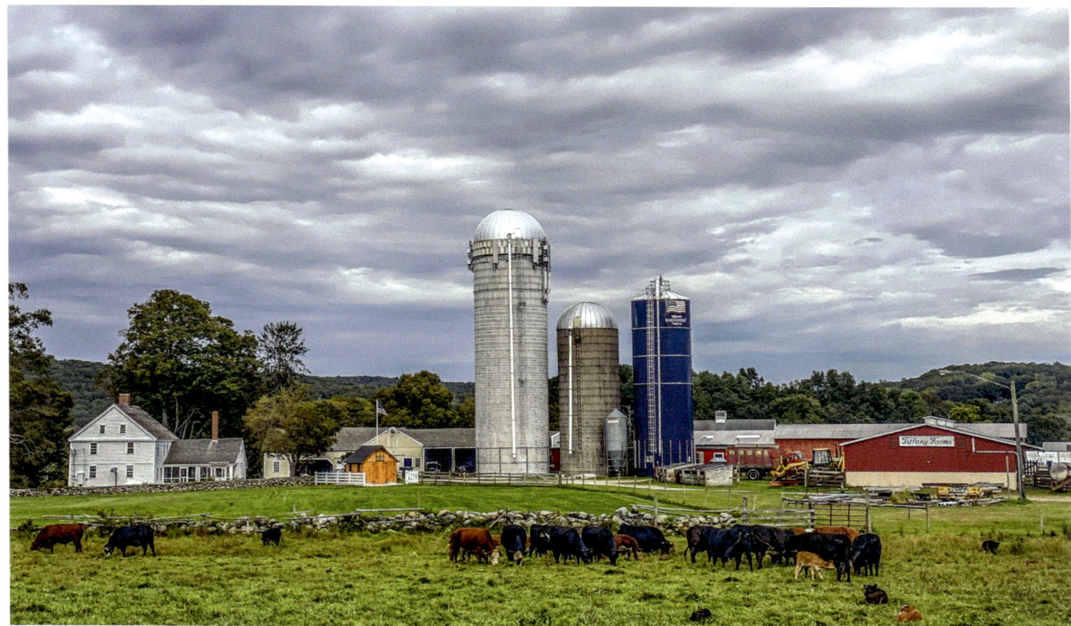

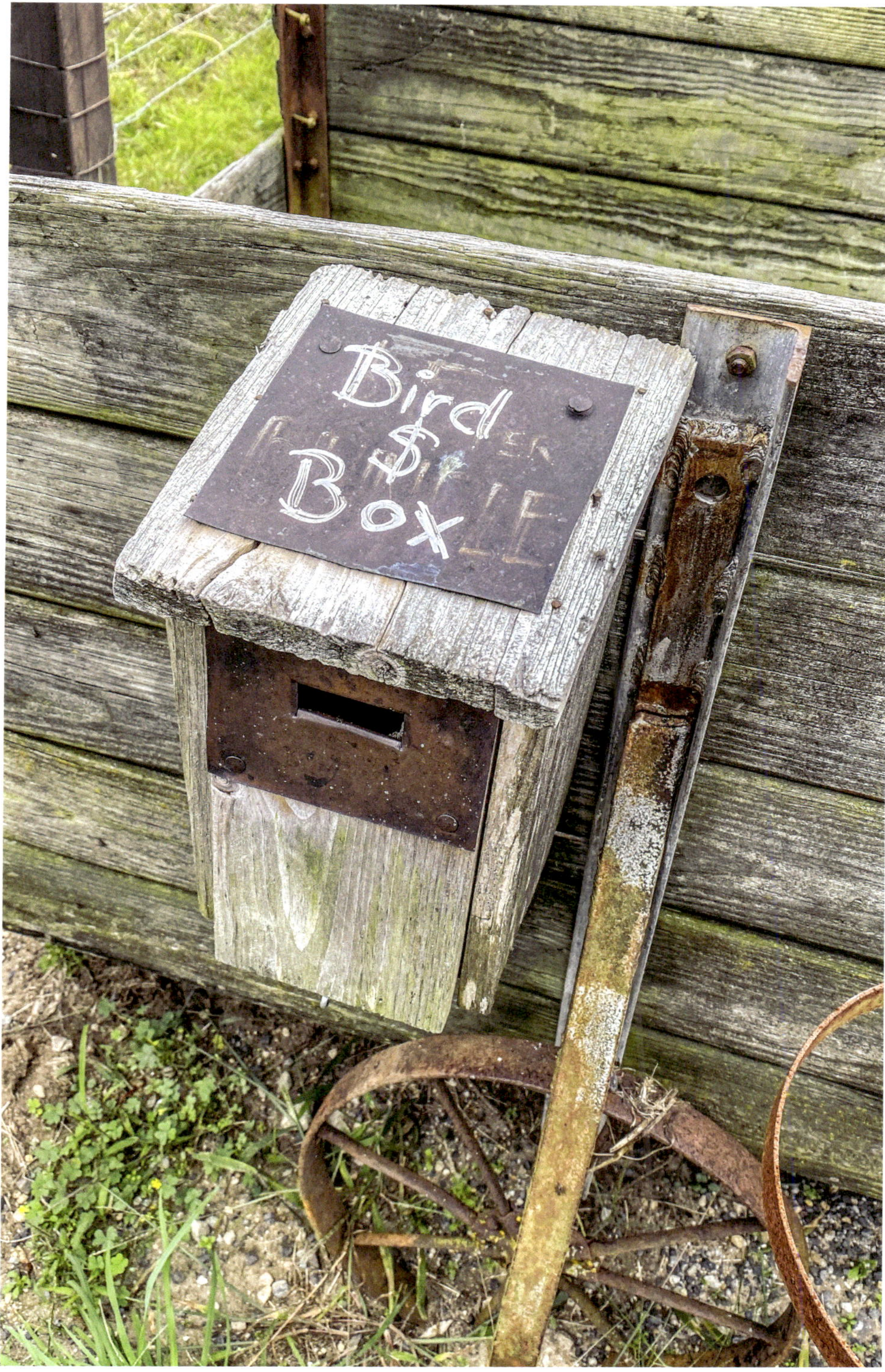
Bird
$
Box

20

Someday Farm, Killingworth

Someday Farm was a project farm with good intentions and vision. A farm like no other, it offered instruction in Kung Fu, Aikido, and Tai Chi. The classic barn provides a home for resting older horses to live out their days. As you mosey through the land, you find the lush green acreage littered with fallen apples, pears, and budding banana trees. Initially, the property was native land and had a sweat lodge, fire pit, and cairns to honor the Lunar polls. The secondary structure is O2 composting with manure, and despite the amount of poop, the air is sweet with the smell of grass. Stephen Watson, aka Shhhhh Dragon, is the Sensei who oversaw the property. Art lines the walls of his dojo. Stephen's art and photography are featured, but others were also welcome to hang there. "Art prolific," the owner states; he doesn't make another piece of art until one sells. Teaching through art and interpretation was part of his lessons with Aikido. Aikido is the martial art of love; one looks at others the way one looks at the self and asks, "Do I want to hurt the self?" Deflection, defense, and physical therapy are factors in Aikido as well. His attempts at making Someday Farm a retreat disappeared when he was diagnosed with cancer. As he fought this horrible disease, his dream had to be sold, as he could no longer care for the farm and teach in the manner that he had. Hopefully, the person who bought the land will continue his dreams and have the best interest in it and its spirit, as Watson did.

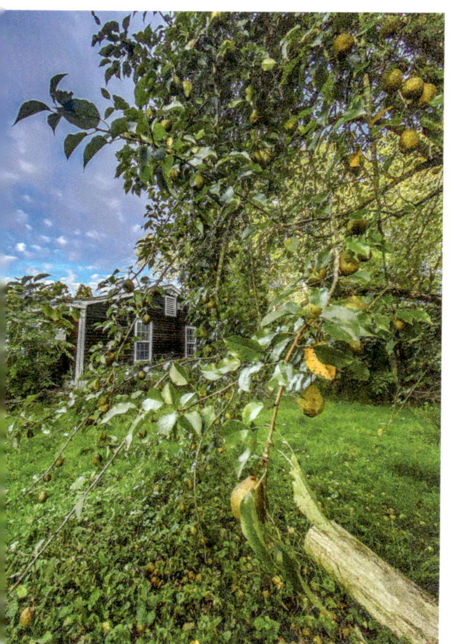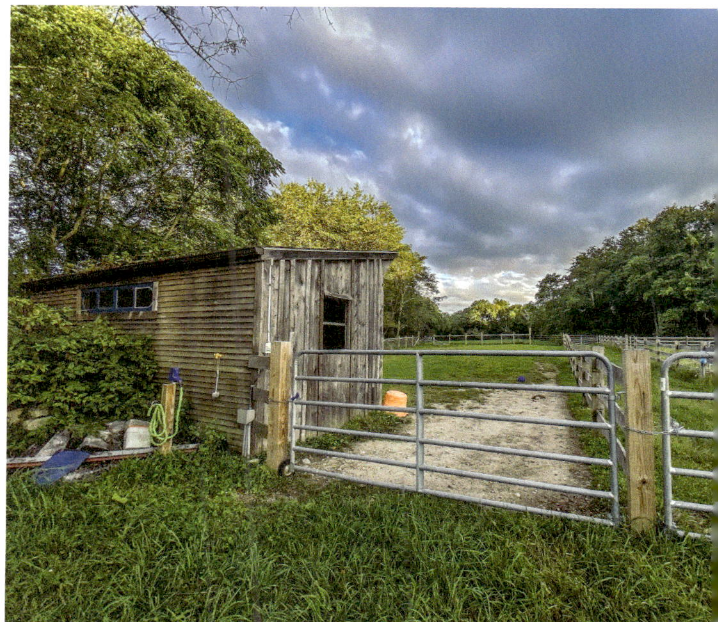

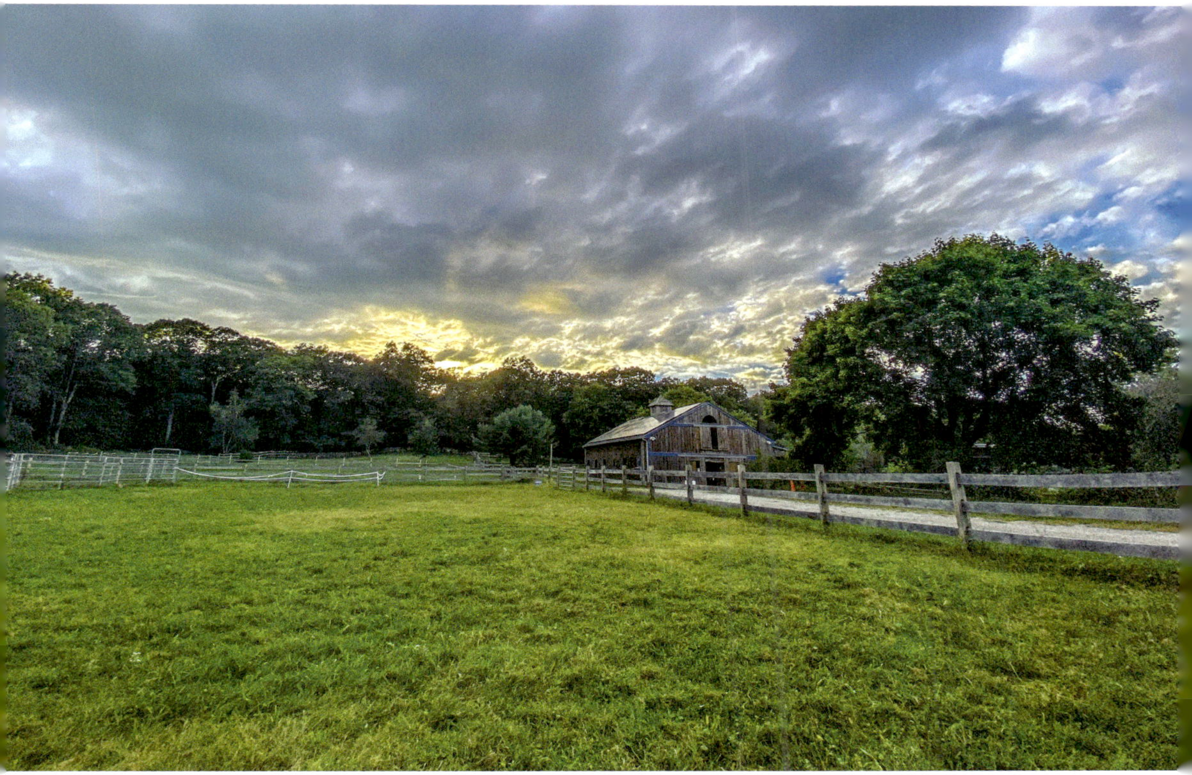

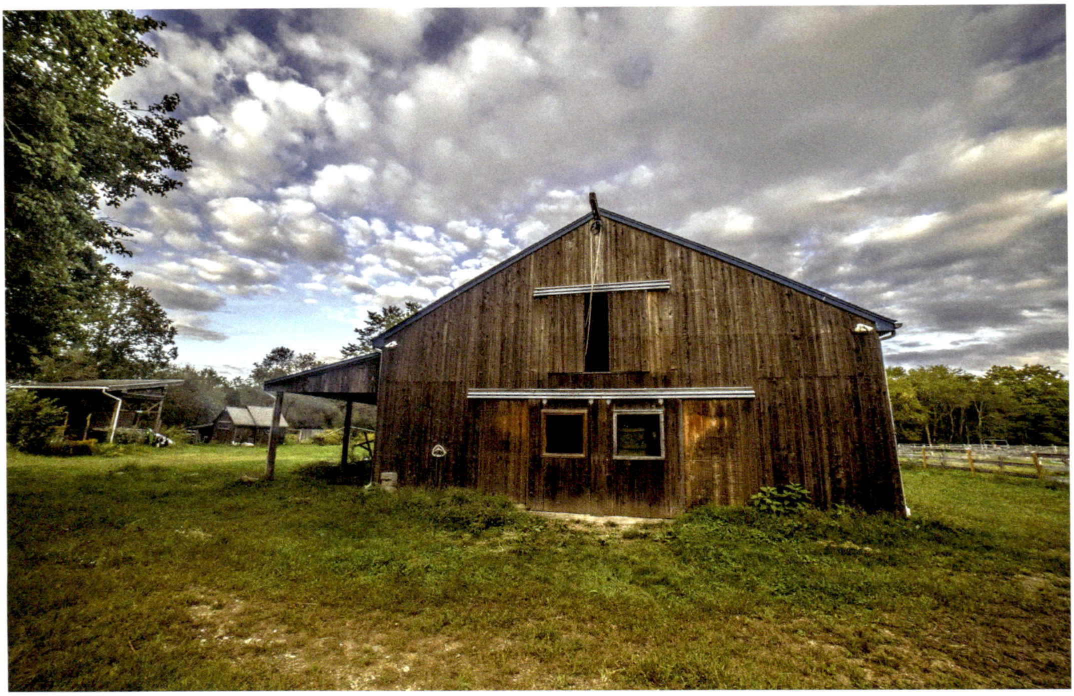

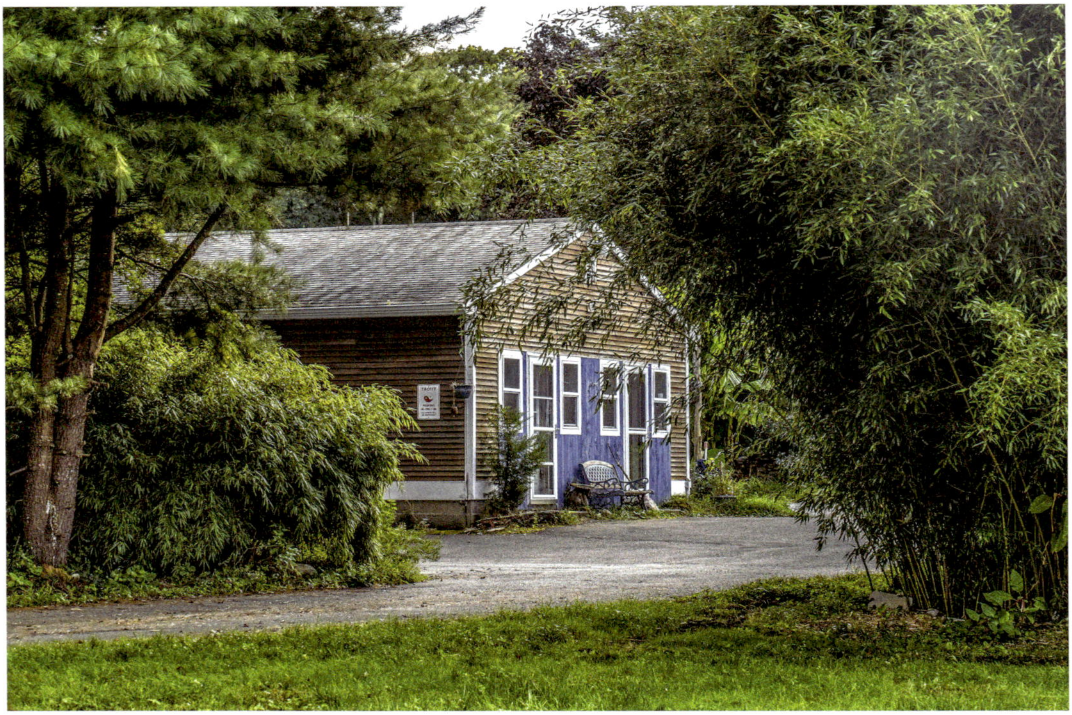

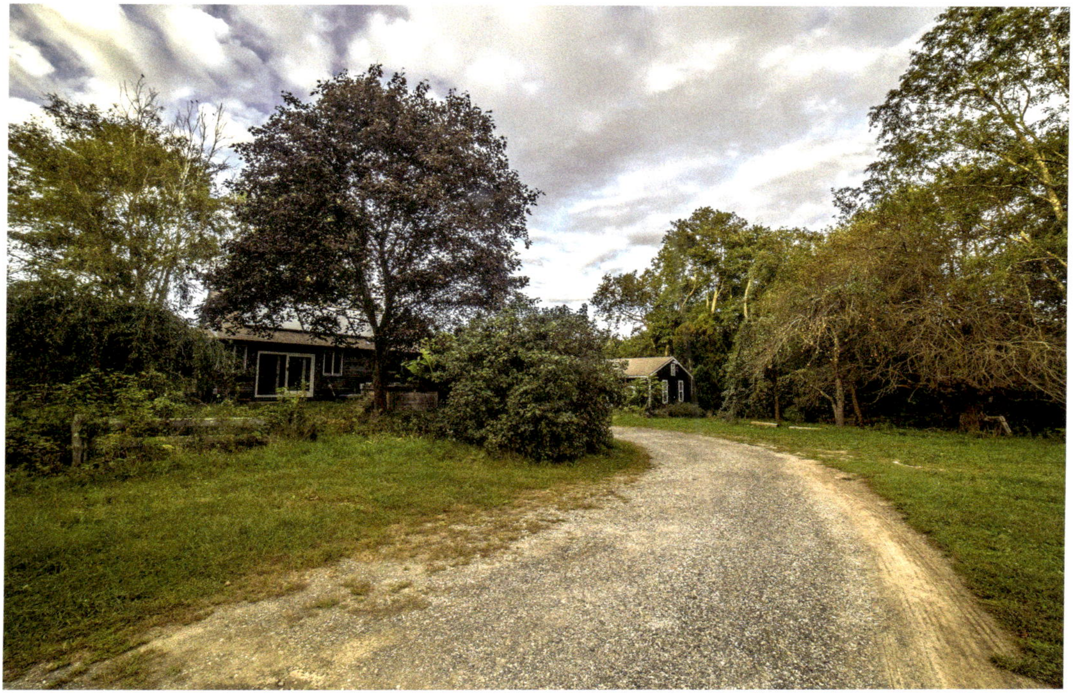

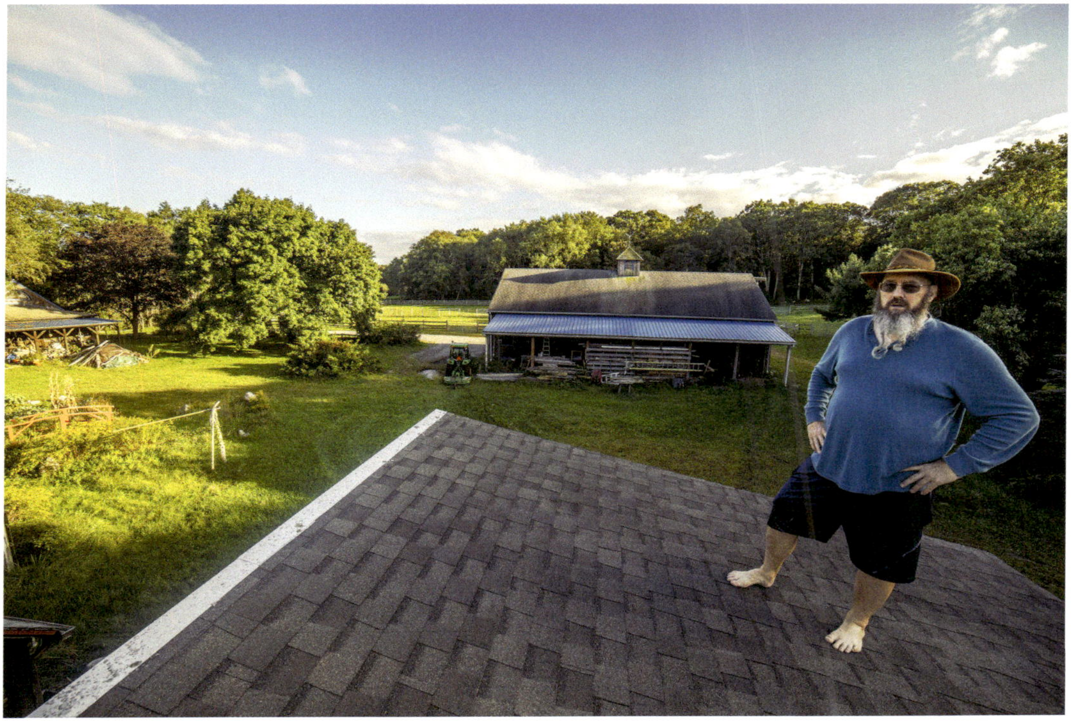

Bibliography

Alpacas, Alpacainfo.com

Arethusa Farm, arethusafarm.com

Aussakita Acres, aussakita-acres.com

Bauer Park, madisonct.org/166/Bauer-Park

Bayler, Ashley, "More than $25K raised for Wallingford farmer burned in 'freak accident,'" *WTNH* (Oct 11, 2023)

Bunnell Farm, bunnellfarm.org

Buttonwood Farm, buttonwoodfarmicecream.com

Calf + Clover, calfandclovercreamery.com

Caron, Matt, Tobacco barns destroyed in Windsor, *Fox61* (June 20, 2019)

Chamard Vineyards, chamard.com

Chester, CT chesterct.org

Connecticut Barns Organization, connecticutbarns.org

CT Visit, Connecticut Barn Trail, ctvisit.com/listings/connecticut-barns-trail

Farmington Food Truck, farmingtonfarmtruck.farm

Grace Farms, gracefarms.org

Greyledge Farm, greyledgefarm.com

Gutierrez, Isa and Lynch, Tara, "Demolished Tobacco Sheds Mark Change in State Agriculture," *NBC Connecticut* (June 17, 2019)

Hale Farm Colebrook, colebrooklandconservancy.org/news

Halfinger Daffodil Farm, halfingerfarms.com

Hilltop Farms, hilltopfarmsuffield.org

Judge, Clark, "Family grateful for community support after robbery shuts down Killingworth farm stand," *HK Now* (August 16, 2021)

Kilgannon, Corey, "Saving the Forgotten Connecticut Farm That Helped Spark M.L.K.'s Dream," *New York Times* (November 12, 2021)

Latella's Piggery, Latellacattleco.wixsite. com

Nagy, Andrew, and Swarzeneggar, "Arnold, Shade in the Dusk; Once the most popular cigar tobacco in the world, genuine Connecticut shade is in danger of disappearing forever," *Cigar Aficionado* (November/December 2019)

New England Alpaca, nealpacas.com

Offgang, Erik, "One of the Country's Oldest Tobacco Farming Families is Turning to

Grains for Beer and Booze," *CT Insider* (August 21, 2018)
Pitt, William, and Sotheby, WilliamPitt.com
Southbury Training School, portal.ct.gov/About-the-Southbury-Training-School
Stacker, stacker.com/connecticut/counties-most-farmland-Connecticut
Tiffany Farms, tiffanyfarmsct.org
Weir Farm, nps.gov/wefa/index.htm
Wicked Tulip Farm, wickedtulips.com

About the Author

Author and photographer Christina Cole had a camera placed in hand at age nine, beginning the most significant romance of her life. Capturing architecture's historic emotional indifference through her lens, showing the variances of gloom and light, makes it impossible not to feel like you were there with her. Her travels have reached remote Alaska, the mountains of Ire, Louisiana boneyard remains, and now to the vast and vacant crumbling ancestry of the North State.